CW01391778

BEYOND THE 'I'

BEYOND THE 'I'

✦

Notes on Waking Up to Oneness

Dhyan Dewyea

iUniverse, Inc.

New York Lincoln Shanghai

BEYOND THE 'I'
Notes on Waking Up to Oneness

Copyright © 2007 by Dhyan Dewyea

All rights reserved. No part of this book may be used or reproduced by any means, graphic, electronic, or mechanical, including photocopying, recording, taping or by any information storage retrieval system without the written permission of the publisher except in the case of brief quotations embodied in critical articles and reviews.

iUniverse books may be ordered through booksellers or by contacting:

iUniverse
2021 Pine Lake Road, Suite 100
Lincoln, NE 68512
www.iuniverse.com
1-800-Authors (1-800-288-4677)

Because of the dynamic nature of the Internet, any Web addresses or links contained in this book may have changed since publication and may no longer be valid.

The views expressed in this work are solely those of the author and do not necessarily reflect the views of the publisher, and the publisher hereby disclaims any responsibility for them.

ISBN: 978-0-595-45901-8 (pbk)
ISBN: 978-0-595-90201-9 (ebk)

Printed in the United States of America

To the one source that IS before eternity starts
and after eternity ends.

Contents

Introduction

The inner search ended rather suddenly and unexpectedly a few years ago, and about two years later I was visiting a mountain town in the American west. Without any intention of doing anything other than going for long walks and exploring the surroundings, one day I experienced an urge to buy a notebook and start writing. The initial impulse was to put into words what awakening is, to phrase it according to how I now saw it, as opposed to how I had imagined it to be.

Starting with those first notes, I revisited a lot of the beliefs that I had previously held, or that I had encountered, on the topic of 'spirituality'. I took another look at some methods of transformation, and at situations that had shaped my journey, and felt that by addressing and questioning them, maybe others would find support when caught up in similar issues.

In the course of reflecting, the text evolved through an interweaving of biographical elements with the questions concerning inner growth and meditation. There are hundreds of texts and many recent ones that address the topic of awakening. I hope that offering additional distinctions may be helpful. I included autobiographical material only to the extent that I wanted to bring attention to certain points, and not primarily to tell a life story.

For the sake of communication, I continue to use the word 'I.' I could have substituted it with 'this being,' 'this body-mind,' but that would have sounded a bit ridiculous. Yet, it is implicit here that 'I' now live with the understanding that this 'I' does not exist and has never existed. Although I might have longed for such direct knowing, I never thought it likely that I would snap out of the limited 'I.' What was in the way was a host of wrong notions, some of which I address in the following.

This book is written with the tacit understanding that language does not reach the realm of truth. This apparent paradox has been stated many times. Put another way, 'who one is' cannot be described in positive terms nor can it be attained. There is only a waking up to what seems hidden that can happen. This text is one invitation among many others to see through the veils that one has accumulated in the form of assumptions concerning others and concerning the self.

1

Enlightenment, Awakening, or Self-Realization?

Increasingly, over the last two decades, in literature as well as spoken conversation, the words enlightenment, awakening, and self-realization have been used interchangeably and as synonyms. Anyone on a spiritual path has probably been exposed to all of them. The intention here is not to give a thorough etymology of each term, or to strive for a 'valid' definition of the terms. The latter is impossible because all of them point to what lies beyond the scope of the definable.

Enlightenment—West meets East

Today's usage of the word enlightenment has two roots. The first goes back to the age of enlightenment—the epoch in history when the rational mind became preponderant. The guiding principle of this period was condensed in Descartes' famous statement, *cogito ergo sum* (I think, therefore I am). It is from this sense that dictionaries give one meaning of 'enlightened' as 'guided by rational thought.'

The other meaning of the word refers to a higher state of consciousness, or even an ultimate state of consciousness. Webster's dictionary describes 'enlightened' in this sense as 'privy to or claiming a sense of spiritual or religious truth.' This latter meaning was adopted into Western language by early 'global' groups such as the theosophists over a century ago through exposure to Eastern culture, especially India.

Beginning then, the notion of 'enlightenment' in the West started to merge with the meaning of the Sanskrit term 'moksha,' the idea that a 'liberated state' or 'buddhahood' is possible as the culmination of embodied existence. Meher Baba and J. Krishnamurti were among the first Easterners of such a stature to travel to the West during the first half of the last century, while at the same time, Westerners traveled East to visit sages like Ramana Maharishi in Arunachala, India. Gradually, the word 'enlightened' got fused to the image of an Eastern 'saint.' These early representatives gave quasi a 'face' to Eastern spirituality, as later did Yogananda and others.

In the heritage of Eastern culture, especially India, the spiritual depth of the inward journey has been explored more than in other cultures. This exploration has greatly influenced contemporary connotations of the understanding of enlightenment in the West. Although the word has become a household term in spiritual circles, I am not aware of it being part of anyone's vocabulary as I grew up. When I was young, we were aware of some mystics such as Meister Eckhart or Hildegard von Bingen, but their *unio mystica* had happened long before during the Middle Ages and within the confines of monasteries, giving it little obvious connection to our modern youthful interests.

In the prevailing context, anyone who is in contact with spiritual groups, or engages in meditation or self-searching, very likely has encountered the notion of enlightenment influenced by the East, and has also likely formed an idea of what such enlightenment may constitute. One may even have met someone, in the East or the West, who is considered enlightened and felt a great showering of love or a luminous radiance from the person. While others were looking for a measure of saintliness in the enlightened one, for a long time, at the very least, I associated it with a powerfully palpable energy field or glistening aura.

If one looks at appearances and outer expressions, and mistakes those appearances as signs of enlightenment, there is quite a danger of comparing oneself. It very easily leads to the belief that 'if this is what being enlightened means, it is completely out of reach. Even though I would deeply like to know myself, I am just a normal person, I am not Buddha, or Ramana, or whoever represents the ideal enlightenment for me.'

Enlightenment became an ideal, and the term has taken on a very loaded meaning. While some masters or teachers mention something to the effect that enlightenment is one's birthright, due to the propensity of comparing oneself, there always looms the common trap of measuring oneself against one's acquired 'enlightenment' idea. One may even believe that one has to morph into someone extra-super-special to fit into it.

Sometimes one hears or reads that 'awakening' is a precursor to 'enlightenment' which is then considered a higher, more perfect, and more complete state. When we adopted the notion of Eastern enlightenment in the West, it was followed by a vast nomenclature of Sanskrit terms, the intricacies of which are often lost in translation—especially if one is not a language scholar. Discussions of key spiritual notions, especially those of Sanskrit origin, can quickly take on an air of thorough hairsplitting. Instead of heaping more knowledge onto the already existing confusion, my remarks are geared towards steering attention to specific beliefs that have already accumulated.

Awakening

The word awakening sounds simple enough, but even this term has been used in different ways. In spiritual contexts, at times it may mean awakening to the sense of inner spaciousness of pure 'am-ness.' At other times, it refers to the discovery of 'being awareness', and again at other times to the recognition of being identical to the absolute, the source of all phenomena. Thus, even the simplicity of the word 'awakening' is a bit deceptive. What it reflects nicely, however, is that just like waking up in the morning, it happens by itself. There is being asleep followed by being awake. The sleeper cannot wake himself or herself up. So when referring to the example of waking up to source, it is my sense that there is nothing gradual about it.

In this latter definition of awakening, everything that was believed about enlightenment goes out the window—for good, by itself, and by default. When all concepts go, enlightenment goes as well. There is a tendency for someone on a spiritual search to build images around the notions of how awakening or enlightenment will occur. This is an attempt at imagining what they are like, hence, one has images about them. Either one is at times thought of in terms of an occurrence of light or energy, or like a large bang, the outcome of which is hoped to be a completely different person from who one was before.

I used to imagine that awakening was an explosion. I do not know where the idea came from, but it was probably generated when others spoke about what had happened to them. I expected it to mean a great rush of energy that would be such a jolt to the body that it would hardly be able to bear it.

There may be an idea that awakening means a complete discontinuity with the past. To use a metaphor, it does not mean that if I had a Volkswagen before, I now wake up and in its place there is a BMW outside the house. There is certainly no sense that one is turned into an instant master. One pervasive and subtle misconception is that it means a change within the scope of the realm of the materially manifest person. This is perhaps more so if a term such as 'illumination' has sunk in and created an inner expectation that one will find him or herself immersed in light.

One aspect of awakening was the surprise that it had nothing to do with acquiring some quality. No change was needed and nothing was gained for the ego, or the person. These were all misconceptions, but I don't know if a more correct view would have speeded up the process.

I have always remembered this statement by a spiritual master. He said, 'Waking up is not difficult, but you keep investing into the false,' that is, the ego. The difficulty is that everyone in one's environment is continuously investing in the false as well; one does not easily know how to stop. One aspect of the 'false' is identifying with one's qualities—with the 'person' aspect. Even after embarking on the inner journey and spending time within spiritual circles, the power of collective myth is not easily overcome. It shows itself, for example, in the assumption that 'awakening' or 'enlightenment' is a state or quality of a higher nature.

Awakening is the realization that the person one took oneself to be has never existed, never had any substance. This is one aspect of what was revealed in self-recognition for 'me', although others prefer to say what is discovered is that there was never an 'independent entity.' It is not an addition of some quality. What is revealed is that there is no such thing as an 'I,' and this was a big surprise. There is no psychological center around which 'I' am constructed, or by which 'this me is caused.' It is impossible for the mind to even attempt to conceive this. I quite like the expression of 'being at source' because it is the realization of being behind, before, and beyond anything that phenomenally and materially appears, and knowing it. One cannot see what is behind the illusion of the 'I,' unless what one takes oneself to be has been completely erased.

Self-Realization

The term self-realization is sometimes used to indicate a self-realized state. This is a manner of speaking, but again, self-realization is not a state. It will not go away, and in fact, the miracle is that it has never gone away, ever!

With the realization of one's truth, or center, existential core, or 'true being,' there is simultaneously the realization that one has always been it. To have gone away from it is revealed as an illusion. Likewise, to come home to it does not involve lugging miles. Nothing is needed except dropping the veils that hide the fact. It has been remarked by many others that it is the realization that what had seemed elusive is actually closer to oneself than anything else, and so it is. What is realized is that one never got even one millimeter away from it. This is why, if one thinks the goal is somewhere else, one is trapped. It never exists 'out there' except from the viewpoint of the illusionary 'I.' The identification with this 'I' makes one look 'out there';

and since 'the there' is already 'the here,' it seems unreachable. The very concept of a search is already a cognitive trap, like a dog trying to catch its tail.

To further complicate the linguistics of the terms, in spiritual literature, we often find the terms 'self' and 'Self,' the first meaning the self as in personality, ego, or 'I,' and the latter meaning the Self of 'true nature.' Dr. Ann Faraday, a psychologist and author of *Dream Power*, says this: "I fell asleep one night in October 1985 and woke the next morning without a self."[1] Her take on the twists of expressing the situation in words is succinctly provocative. She writes, "I would like to see the term Self with a capital S: Self-actualisation, Self-realisation, Self-transcendence—expunged from psychological and spiritual literature, reserving the word strictly for the empirical self of everyday life. It is the whole obfuscating concept of self which needs to be transcended, for in my experience there has never really been any self to transform, actualise, realize or transcend."[2]

The 'no-self-realization' is not a realization in the sense that either a 'self' or 'no-self' is brought into existence or made real; it is a realization only in the sense of becoming aware of no-self. It is more like a 'NoSelf—NoRealization'. If this realization does not depend on bringing anything into existence, or making anything 'real,' could it then be possible to be less in conflict with the 'self,' investing less into changing and conditioning the perceived but non-existent self?

2

What Is Awakening?

When someone discovers in awakening that there is no 'I' or self, either before or after, one also discovers there is no one who can awaken. It is therefore wrong to say 'I am awake'—whatever is cannot be had by anyone.

Implosion of the Subject-Object Structure

It has been said that to awaken is a universal accident or an act of grace.[3] I like to call it a cognitive accident. It is a leap in perspective, and based on my experience over the years, it was clear that 'I' could not do the leaping. I used to experience this as the ultimate dilemma and got pretty exasperated at times. The paradox is this: no effort, no path, leads directly to it because we function from the standpoint of a subject with the world as an object.

The role of masters, teachers, and guides has been to bring about realization generally through unexpected devices because it is not possible to bring it about through deduction. Zen masters are said to know when a disciple is ripe for the decisive hit of the Zen stick. Some have been said to sneak into the room of a sleeping disciple in the middle of the night, and jump on the fellow while shouting, 'Wake up!' Maybe, the disciple then realizes 'the goose is out.'

'The goose is out' refers to a famous Zen koan by Master Nansen. Reportedly, he was asked how a gosling that had grown in a bottle can be taken out without breaking the bottle. Nansen is said to have clapped his hands and remarked, 'See, the goose is out.' This simply means that one's true nature has never been contained in the small vessel (bottle) of the personality (the ego). It was always the other way round: the bottle was always empty.

But the paradox is that the only direction we can look is inside, within 'us,' right into the complexities that constitute our apparent 'I's or personalities. Sufis say that God hid himself in the most remote place possible, in the very center of a person's heart, where he is most difficult to find. At that center, there is no movement, there is no inward and no outward, no container and nothing contained—no bottle and no goose.

In contradiction to my lifelong habit of extending all kinds of efforts to get to some 'truth,' one aspect of the so-called awakening is its utter simplicity. Because it is so simple, so close to oneself, and so effortless, how could it be missed at all, if not for all the identifications of being a someone? I have had to wonder if there aren't people who have fallen into it and have simply forgotten because it is so unspectacular, as well as a tremendous relief. I also could not help wondering if the significance of it could be missed by someone who is not somewhat educated in such matters. Just recently, I read how H. W. L. Poonja supposedly had an awakening at the age of 8 or 9 but did not put it into perspective until he met Ramana Maharshi when he was around 30 years old.

Quite likely, I am not the only person who used to imagine that the occurrence of awakening is like an explosion, but rather than being an energetic occurrence, it is a matter of cognition. It is, rather, an implosion. The subject and object of the ego-structure both collapse together. Because of the identification with the false "I"-subject up to that point, it is impossible to willfully bring this collapse about. Instead, at least it was my experience that there were times when I fervently fought perceived threats to 'my I.' All attempts to disidentify from it felt like annihilation—such was the entanglement.

The Zen nun Chiyono is noted to have said "No Water, No Moon" when the bottom fell out of her pail and the water splashed to the ground. In the Zen tradition, this sentence exemplifies her moment of enlightenment. There was nothing left to reflect the moon. That which reflects disappears together with that which is reflected. The I and the object disappear together. What is beyond is called 'pure subjectivity,' which again is just another phrase meaning source.

Beyond the Subject-Object Structure

It is impossible to describe truth, source, self-knowledge, et cetera, because for one, our western language is based on the subject-object relationship, and second, a word can at best be a pointer to what it signifies. Specifically concerning this topic, if there is no subject relating to an object, what can be said? I could say that the nature of things is that 'love responds to love.'[4] Logically, this is an absurd statement, like a snake biting its tail. It is a redundant remark. Maybe the statement can be taken in a poetic way, but from the viewpoint of logic, it is not a meaningful statement. Yet, it does point to what is—there is nothing outside of love; there is nothing outside of the divine, if you will. When the subject and object both collapse, they are both revealed as immaterial, illusionary, as not possessing substance on their own. It is like falling behind them, into a center of eternity that is made of no other thing than bliss, everything arising out of it and subsiding into it.

This kind of bliss is not a state that can come and go and turn into despair. It is not dependent on some condition. This bliss is what one is, fundamentally. As water is liquid, one's nature is bliss by definition. Because the word bliss may evoke all kinds of ideas, I like to describe it as intrinsic deliciousness. It is not an event, an emotion or a feeling; on that level, it is not an experience that can turn into its opposite. It always is, behind the suffering, the excitement, the boredom, or any other state. It is not the temporary sense of ecstasy which can happen to anyone along the way. Hence, when any feeling, no matter how great it has been, is leaving again, it is best to let it go without resistance.

Identification and its Root

Identification with a body is the first attachment. Because identification with the body well as its emotions and mental activity is so strong, the process of disidentification seems increasingly threatening to the ego-structure as well as its world view; its collapse is not easily brought about. To work our way through all the layers of 'what we think we are' is no spring outing. Sometimes the process of disidentification seems easy: 'This is what I have believed so far; hmm, it may not really be like that.' Sometimes it feels like death and one fights the process tooth and nail. Saying 'I am not the body' sounds easy enough until emotional reactions to an illness or pain occur.

The body is identified with a name in childhood. Everyone takes oneself to be the person who lives in this body, or is this body. This is at the root of what we call conditioning. Everything that happens from then on is seen through the lens of a 'me' to whom it happens. But this 'I' notion is fuzzy from the get go. The 'I' is taken to be a complex of behaviors, feelings, and mental concepts that are seen as attached to a body—one believes oneself to be living in the body and to be its attachments.

Being in society, as all of us are, we are automatically and constantly classified by name, gender, age, and other attributes of the body. Mostly one responds in kind by accepting the classification and extending it to others. One may say 'you don't see me correctly, I am so instead of so,' showing preference for one classification over another, but the identification with classification is still operable nevertheless. Most people do not know how to be without such classifications at all.

Even within the spiritual communities, there is a great deal of classifying that goes on. One classifies oneself and another according to the preferred teaching or path, according to psychological notions, or according to notions of a spiritual growth ladder. This constant labeling can even feel like an aggression, and just as equally, a constant dance between letting go of one's identifications and being reclassified by others.

Within the spiritual context there are plenty of discussions about whether there is really a seeker and a path that the seeker is 'on.' Both are labels which people tend to identify with and invest in to varying degrees. It is easy to see, in this example, how a label such as 'seeker' turns the 'I' subject into an object—one sees oneself as a something, and becomes 'someone who....' The eternal question 'who am I?' is meant to lead out of identifications with such labels.

The Dilemma

Nowadays there are substantial amounts of not just traditional scriptures, but also contemporary writings that speak about awakening and explain it by saying one is already what one seeks. But statements such as 'You are that,' 'This is it,' or 'Just this!' are usually not understood. If they were, one would have to hear them only once and that would be the end of the search. Upon hearing such statements, the 'this' is experienced exactly as the particular condition one is suffering from, wants to get away from, feels imprisoned by. How can it therefore be the answer, let alone freedom or ultimate fulfilment?

If 'this' is it, and at the same time 'this' is experienced as the lack and struggle, then how can 'this' be 'it'? There is agreement that whatever is dubbed 'source', 'Self,' 'absolute,' and so forth, cannot be put into words because it is not an object; thus the word 'this' is as good as any since all words—even 'inconceivable'—fall short.

It is often added that 'this' is not the mind. I always felt thrown into a loop by it. It is not that I cared so much about the idea of mind; I cared about the one I struggled with, my own, and not about a general notion of mind as such, or how that differed from the idea of universal mind, or someone else's definition of mind. Is it not one's own mind that one wants to get relief from, or get out from? Hearing statements such as 'You are that' sometimes felt like an attempt at consolation, like being thrown a bare bone. Usually, a sentence like 'you are not the mind' followed on its heel. But 'mind' is such a general and abstract term. To distinguish what mind is and what mind does is not easy, especially when said mind presents itself as the tool for its own diagnosis.

The Idea of Oneness

The statement 'You are that' is now generally accepted as the core statement for a growing number of followers of the non-duality path known as Advaita, or in its more contemporary form, neo-Advaita. For a long time into my own journey, I had either not encountered or paid attention to the term Advaita; if I did, it seemed like some philosophy. I had come across the 'who am I' question early on; it had been of great experiential and practical value and had early on been a guidance for the inner focus. I had no idea that it was central to the teaching of Ramana Maharshi, in fact until very recently I had no idea who he was or that the 'who am I' question was his main teaching, or that he had anything to do with Advaita.

From the mid-nineties onward, there were a few occasions when I accompanied a friend to a talk by someone who was said to be awakened and noticed that, more and more often, the idea of oneness was communicated. To me, it meant nothing; not only because it was of no utilitarian value, but because I wanted to know who I was and was unconcerned with a oneness that I conceived to be somewhere else. The idea of oneness seemed philosophical, and I had no intention of convincing myself that it was true, when simultaneously my real experience was different. On occasion, when I heard someone talk about being 'this,' I usually wondered what frame of mind that person was in before they knew 'this' or before they knew oneness. There was a degree of astonishment because I was still carrying the image of enlightenment as an exceedingly rare occurrence; now all of a sudden so many seemingly normal people were spiritually awake.

Advaita or non-duality as a cognized approach was an idea that was absent from my path. Its Sanskrit twin of yoga, in the sense of union, always seemed impenetrably mysterious. I did not care about finding oneness, I cared about finding out who I was. So it was a bit of a surprise that one aspect of the discovery of 'awakening' was the revelation of the underlying unity of all that is, not as a philosophical or intellectual understanding, but as a direct and existential knowing.

Some people wake up and find their selves gone; for others, including me, a substantial amount of uncovering, of going inside, the so-called journey, has to happen—a preparation for what needs no preparation, but being at the same time, no preparation for what is always present within the very preparation. The notion of a journey is a paradox because believing we are someone else other than we are is also a paradox.

3

Searching

Whether someone calls it oneness or true self, when something is hidden, an amount of uncovering seemingly has to happen. This uncovering has a lot to do with what is believed. In order to show a few notions on which I had gotten stuck, it may be illustrative to revisit some examples from my biography. It is my impression that the same key ideas, being historically shaped, are influencing a number of people including those who are engaged with spirituality of the Advaita or Zen kind, and who may even share similar experiences. While Advaita has somewhat become the method du jour, I nevertheless detect a kind of cross over—the same people being interested in meditation and the 'who am I' question on one hand, and engaging with and thinking in terms of self-development on the other. I hope a certain contrasting of both will prove fruitful.

Although some biographical events are described below, this is done with the understanding that biographical events are not the 'cause' of the cognition of never having been that biography. 'Snapping out of it' means finding oneself at home in the uncaused. Only the uncaused can be the cause of anything, hence, no matter what happens within the life story, the latter cannot be cause of the uncaused, being its effect.

Discovering Self-Discovery

While attending university in Germany in the early seventies, there was still the emancipatory and transformatory spirit that had erupted in the sixties. This historical epoch left its mark on psychology like it did on other areas of life. For me, there was an early involvement in psychological exploration of the time, largely corresponding to the then favored experimental approach to psychological and therapeutic techniques.

For example, psychoanalysis had been available to only a few due to the tremendous investment in time and money which it required, and was by then considered too long-winded and tedious, if not elitist. It was being replaced by self-discovery groups. Psychological methods and psychotherapy became democratized and widely available to those interested. So-called New Psychology or Humanistic Psychology was within my radar in university, having reached Europe from the United States.

When the first Gestalt psychology group was announced in our town under the leadership of an American therapist who had worked with Fritz Perls, I had a strong pull to participate. I remember quite vividly how just before the start of the five day process, internalized parental messages showed up as arguments against attending. Before I actually walked through the door of the group room, I experienced an increasing inner squeeze of confusion and doubt; I could hardly breathe. Not surprisingly, my work within the group had to do with elements of decision making and aspects of it were about pleasing a parent. As I emerged from the process five days later, for the first time ever, I was not thoroughly cut off from my emotions. In as much as there is a well-formed self-image in young adulthood, it had been more than shaken up. A lid had been taken off accumulated hurts, insecurities, and anger; my unconscious survival strategy had mostly been to relegate all emotions into the shadows because I did not know how to deal with them and because there was a taboo around them in my family of origin.

Around that time, Alexander Lowen's book *Bioenergetics* was a big hit.[5] It was more than evident to me how repressed emotions impeded breathing and caused muscle tension (called 'body armor' by Lowen). It was not long before a local group which provided bio-energetic exercises was formed. The exercises were work, but through their particular combination of posture and breathing, they allowed for substantial releases of physical and emotional tension.

We wholeheartedly threw ourselves into experimenting with such new methods because a genuine interest in our inner workings guided those endeavors. Outside the scope of academic psychology, one new approach was that of Transactional Analysis.[6] It taught us to distinguish between whether we speak and act from one of three ego states—child, adult, or parent—and how the emotional aspect of the interaction often belies spoken words.

We rediscovered our emotions, not so much as a result of a conscious decision, but because it was a collective need—we wanted to bring anything that had been repressed to the surface. Some friends even participated in a three week program of Janov's 'Primal Scream,' a process intended to open up the emotions of early childhood. Another went to the United States to study the deep tissue work of Rolfing, pursuing the connection of body and emotion further. Meanwhile, self-discovery became a movement. It spawned new methods, group leaders, and growth centers such as Esalen in the United States and Zist in Germany.

There was a sense of adventure, even as we faced our rages and hurts. We challenged each other's facades, called each other on the falseness of the 'nice girl, nice guy' image. In a collective effort, we needed and wanted to look at what was behind the social masks. Later on in the seventies, this evolved into encounter groups, where the superficiality of false polite-ness took a back seat to confrontation; participants screamed at each other and let raw emotions pour out, but afterwards, they also experienced a depth of connection with the other that had previously been unknown. At the time, intensity ruled; there was one thing we did not want, and that was to feel dead.

Over time, implicitly or explicitly, an understanding took hold that such activities were meant to expose and crack our egos instead of just healing past hurts. What drove me initially towards some of the available methods was that at times, I felt my emotions and inner world were like a prison. Like many people, I often did not know what I was feeling, only that it was often uncomfortable. It was as if I was sitting on a mountain of locked-in energy that needed to be freed. But after a while, self-discovery took us only that far. While repressed stuff had been uncovered and there had been a certain unburdening, something was missing.

Traveling to the East

Another aspect of that era was an increasing interest in East-ern culture. I never forget how a book on Zen Buddhism by Erich Fromm impacted me when a teenager. For the first time ever I saw the word 'dhyana'; it was explained by the author to be the etymological root of Zen. I remember sitting in my room, on the floor, unable to think anything but 'this (dhyana) is my name'. This was the first time that a dimension of the mysterious and unexplainable came to the fore of conscious-ness. Ten years later, the previous incident all but forgotten, an Eastern master addressed me with that name. One meaning of dhyana, often also translated as meditation, refers to the path of discernment, and much later it became evident to what extent that impulse, or natural knack, asserted itself. As East-ern traditions found their way into collective Western experi-ence, illustrated early on by the photos of the Beatles with Maharishi Yogi, something new was in the air. There was a his-torical shift taking place as increasing numbers of people set out towards the East.

From the first stirrings of what could be called an inner search, I never felt that it had been a matter of choice—it was what liv-ing brought, it was how things went. I entered into psychologi-cal exploration because it seemed the task at hand. While it brought some release, some insights, and the resurfacing of an old childhood trauma, constrictive personality patterns were still quite bothersome. All the while, there was a much more deeply hidden inner place that seemed to be calling and to which all the psychological methods I had undergone up to that time did not reach.

In a sense, there was a searching going on. It was like being urged back to some place for which there was no word. I would not have called myself a seeker as this label seemed intellectually dry, almost superficial. It did not quite reflect the somewhat passionate quality of what was driving me—to the utter dismay of some friends and family. At the time, I also would not have related to the saying that it was the sense of separation I was trying to remedy, since such separation is often considered the motivation for 'seeking.' Instead, what I felt was a 'deeper' center somewhere within, something that was simply calling out, some place I felt was there and where I wanted to get.

Everyone probably has a sense that certain greater events or turns in their lives were not brought on by them, that they rather occurred to them. Through this kind of impetus, in my late twenties, I found myself standing on a curb in Bombay waiting for a bus with a distinct wondering of how this had happened, despite having lived through many months during which my internal reasoning resisted and argued against such a journey as the intensely-felt inner pull finally won out.

At the time, traveling to the East had become a collective phenomenon. It had to do with looking for an inner dimension that was, in a more or less conscious way, understood as spiritual. The word 'ego' had come into focus at the time, in the sense of something rather undesirable, even though there was little conscious reference to what was behind that ego. Also, notions of enlightenment had started drifting into our consciousness, which up to that time, had not been such a staple idea in Western culture. I doubt whether prior to this time, many in the West knew the word 'satsang,' as ubiquitous as it has become nowadays. Personally, I do not specifically remember when I first encountered the notion of enlightenment, or with regard to which 'enlightened being,' but it resonated with a dimension preciously close to heart, invoking the sense of the living presence of a Love Supreme.

Ideas of Enlightenment

Individually and collectively, traveling to India had something to do with wanting to know what enlightenment was. Over time, all kinds of ideas formed around it in my mind.

For example, theories about the psychosomatic roots of illnesses had become popular in Germany in the seventies. Influenced by them, I thought that if most illnesses have psychosomatic roots, how can an enlightened being get cancer? The facts are that he or she can, and often has. Another early idea of mine was that an enlightened being will not feel emotions, and this is an idea I have encountered at times, even lately, amongst some spiritually interested people. Some people believe an enlightened person cannot have sex, or cannot smoke. Some believe he is God, or at least someone who is imbued by God (or a divine energy) to a greater extent than the rest of us.

Shortly after arriving in India, someone told me about an old enlightened woman with the name Hazrat Babajan who was considered to be the master of Meher Baba. I could hardly believe it; that a woman could be enlightened was big news to me!

Many years later, I met the founder of a popular method of inquiry in a small group setting on the east coast of the United States. I remember her speaking about not being able to function 'properly' in a practical way after having her awakening. I believe she said that afterwards, for a brief time, she forgot how to dress. After her presentation, the thought that sneaked in was that 'if waking up means kind of "losing it," if it means not being able to function at all anymore, is it worth it?'

One belief that was floating around then was that there would be a discontinuity with the past in the sense of having one 'I' prior, and a completely different 'I' after enlightenment. Some people, including myself, thought that being 'enlightened' meant having a certain charisma that can be felt, something akin to having a very strong energy field. With such an idea, there is usually then a comparison—one compares oneself with someone who is considered very special and unique or even buddha-like, and predictably, one does not seem to have what it takes.

Almost everyone who is somewhat interested in this topic has, in one way or another, acquired concepts about something called enlightenment. I remember that one of the stories I heard in India was that the expecting mother of a future enlightened one dreams of a white elephant during pregnancy. Well, my mother certainly did not have such a dream, so it was rather devastating to see my deepest longings squashed, at least for this lifetime. Having encountered the notion of enlightenment in an Eastern context, in those days, I had sort of a half-conscious belief that without being born in India, one did not have a chance.

It is best to not let one's outlook be clouded by such concepts. A warning light should come on when fantasies or images about 'what enlightenment is' start to encroach. It is better to recognize these fantasies and images and the multiple ways in which they can appear. Such ideas are traps; they invariably point to something which is 'out there somewhere else.' One needs to be wary because these ideas can live in one's mind below the conscious radar.

If some of the ideas mentioned sound naive, it is because a lot of them are. Instead of downplaying their potency, it is important to address them. It may be very useful to release such ideas out into the open, for example, by sharing them in a small group, or asking, 'what does everyone think enlightenment is like?' I venture a wild guess that no one is without such ideas. The exercise might be very fruitful in helping others let go of such ideas by bringing them out into the light.

One will find that most of these concepts imply that enlightenment is a quality that someone has. The connotations around such a quality run the gamut from being supremely desirable to being completely out of reach. Sometimes they can be somewhat frightening, for example, as conveyed by the notion of the 'death of the ego.' Some connotations revolve around being holy. Some are based on how an enlightened one looks like or how he should be living, for example as a solitary celibate saint in a Himalayan cave. Some highlight the idea that enlightenment is the fruit of decades of meditation, past lives spent as a Tibetan monk, or of being someone specifically chosen or extra special.

The common thread to most of these concepts is that 'enlightenment' is a quality that has to be attained, and furthermore, in most cases, that it is a quality that is almost impossible for a 'normal' person to attain. I remember just a few years ago, a good friend talking almost incredulously about the fact that a woman she had known a long time ago was now considered 'enlightened' (the woman never called herself 'enlightened' to my knowledge). There were obviously preconceived ideas about enlightenment, how it should look like and who can have it. Not long afterwards, I had a very similar reaction while watching Irina Tweedie[7] on TV during an interview. She looked like a lovable gentle senior citizen, she seemed so normal. At the time, I still thought how could such an evidently normal woman be enlightened?

Enlightenment as Koan

Awakening to source means identification with a personal 'I' and its qualifications has ceased. The answer to the question 'who am I?' is not 'I am enlightened.' Enlightenment cannot be an attribute of a person because what it refers to is the realization that the personal 'I' is an illusion; the no-self does not have any qualities at all.

A couple of Zen koans come to mind, specifically, 'What is your face before your grandparents were born?' and, 'There is a gosling in the bottle, how to get it out?' These questions seem to take the respondent far away from the answer which is being sought, they seem to trick the mind into a search that roams far and wide even though the purpose of such koans is to bring about an existential opening or insight into who the respondent is. Similarly, the quest for a quality called 'enlightenment' seems to lead far away from what is, because this quality is basically non-existent and therefore remains elusive—like chasing a Fata Morgana.

Maybe the fairy tale of enlightenment has been invented for the same reason that Zen Buddhism invented koans. While identified with the 'I,' it is impossible to see either the nature of that 'I' or the nature of being. Perhaps 'enlightenment' is just such a koan that sends one even further away in order to produce a dead end from which an existential satori is the only answer, a satori on the nature of what is sought, which of course is the one who is seeking in the first place.

4

Hoping to Find

Can it be assumed that whatever inner journey one follows is exactly the appropriate one, exactly the right one for one's individual condition? Some wake up in the morning and are spiritually awake; others, who knows for what reasons, travel to foreign places. Some meet a master while some are guided by life only. For some it seems easy and for others it is a lot of work. Not only this, there is also the challenge of never knowing what unfolds next when one is on the path, something that Irina Tweedie expresses here: "The problem with the spiritual path is you know how you begin, but you never know how you end. It is like putting your foot in a wasp's nest."[8]

The Search—a Roller Coaster Ride

Immersion in Eastern culture, India in particular, brought a host of new experiences on many levels, not only for myself, but for a whole wave of other Westerners who headed East. The new sights and smells alone catapulted one into a different frame of mind. There were the challenges of constant physical adjustment, and a heretofore unknown 'spiritual' quality permeating the very air and soil of the surroundings. For the first time ever, my soul felt at home.

There were many meetings with people of spiritual stature and fragrance, some of whom I saw as enlightened. And there were meetings with many other travelers from different countries around the world who were also looking for a spiritual dimension. There was increased experimentation with different approaches to meditation and entering into deeper levels of meditative experiences. There was a definite widening of the scope of experience, with the inner being thriving while the body as well as emotions, suffered a roller coaster of ups and downs. I had not known the English word 'bliss' till then, let alone what it could possibly mean. Soon, brought on by different, sometimes intensely structured, meditation processes and other awareness exercises, I got a taste of it.

Sometimes states of intense inwardness occurred with a natural spontaneity that I had not known in my previous life in the West. It was enchanting and mysterious, and at times, devastating and scary. Deep fears and tears would arise seemingly out of nowhere. There could be a sense of bottomless aloneness in the midst of fellow meditators, or a new dimension of lovingness, if not the taste of universal love itself. It was, at the same time, a sense of coming home and a sense of being utterly put through the wringer. I used to say that it was like someone cleaning out all the chakras along the sushumma (the channel of energy along the spine) with one of those old fashioned bottle brushes which were used in my childhood in Germany for cleaning milk bottles. It could at times be as unpleasant as this metaphor implies. The fast vibrating energy quality of the surroundings also acted as a catalyst for numerous inner processes. Yes, there was at times a very deep inner calm, but it was usually quickly followed by some inner upheaval.

If a certain curiosity is evoked about what some of the inner experiences of that time specifically were, before I answer, let me turn the question back, and in the spirit of the 'who am I' question, ask: 'For whom does the desire to know more appear; who wants to know more of a story?' At this point, these former experiences are memories, but I will list a few: A very enhanced dream activity; spontaneous remembrance of past life situations; the body being so energized that it went without sleep for days; and a heat sensation in the third eye area (sixth chakra) that lasted for months. Sometimes there was a sense of love that dissolved old inner knots in occasional floods of tears. Once, for about ten days, whenever I sat down, the whole body started shaking, and fortunately, neither myself nor others around me were concerned by this.

In hearing about such inner experiences, especially of the more 'esoteric' ones, there is a danger of comparing and for someone to think 'I did not experience this but I should, need, or want to'; or retrospectively, one may think 'such and such an experience is nothing extraordinary, I had better ones.' This is why I hesitated to even mention them, and why I feel a more detailed account would be inappropriate. Some older spiritual traditions, for example the Sufis, keep aspects of the inner dimensions hidden, reserving them for the teaching realm of a master and his or her disciple alone. This is probably a precaution to prevent pointless comparisons that lead nowhere.

To Whom Does the Search Happen?

Over time, a burning longing lodged itself into the heart, though in hindsight, I do not recall that this occurred at one specific point in time. It was a physical sensation that at times got rather intense and even hard to bear. Whatever was happening, calling it a search is an afterthought, a rather abstract attempt at giving a name to a dynamic unfolding that was not consciously brought on by me. It was something I could not help but live, in other words, it seemed to occur to me rather than by and through me.

These days it is often said that there is not really a seeker since one never was a separate independent individual, that the whole idea of a search is nothing but a game the divine is playing with itself. But in such a statement, the recognition of an end result is taken as the starting point. To get there, it is more than likely that the phenomenal and temporal body-mind (at all its levels) is impacted to different degrees. There are often experiences of an inner, emotional, and energetic kind that happen within the dynamic of the search or path and are quickened by it. Irina Tweedie was tasked by her guru to keep a diary, and her resulting autobiography is a very informative account of inner phenomena that were brought on by the particular impact of her training on her particular body-mind.

Along similar lines, friends who were followers of J. Krishnamurti gave little room to an address of inner states. With some of those friends, it felt that such topics were almost taboo, as I sensed they had a preference towards a more mental approach. I was therefore rather surprised when I read, not long ago in Jayakar's[9] biography, how Krishnamurti himself underwent an extended period during which his body-mind system was greatly affected by energetic occurrences. Whether these are called mystical experiences or awakenings, they obviously preceded his later mental clarity and reflect the specific way in which his body/mind/soul was impacted by the process. Still, I get the sense that lovers of his writings tend to dismiss these occurrences. While allowing for individual differences and conceding that people who are drawn to Krishnamurti may not need to go through a lot of emotional/energetic experiences or upheavals, the journey itself often does bring such phenomena about within the temporally manifest being.

The statement that there is no search or no path is an expression of the overall paradox. In order to understand it, one requires understanding, and this often presupposes a path which consists of solely mental cognition. This path is clearly favored by some, but for others, vivid energetic effects are either a starting point or stations along the way.

For example, I needed bio-energetics before I could even think of meditation, and when still in college, needed to trudge off a hundred times in the early morning for Osho's dynamic meditation.[10] I did not do this because I was 'seeking,' but because the flow of breathing felt constricted and this meditation helped loosen it. Jean Klein's saying that "the motive behind all effort is to be effortless" applied here.[11] The question is not so much 'what' is the right path, or 'is there one,' but 'to whom' is all this occurring?

The Truth Is not in Experiences

While the scope of the familiar, habitual, German-bred 'I' became a bit softer and was altered by many new experiences, a belief that the truth was equivalent with a *specific* experience of a supremely satisfying nature began to gain a foothold. No matter how many experiences there were, there was a hope for 'the one' that would bring an 'enlightenment' that would not go away an hour later. Of course, it is logically absurd to look for a permanent experience, since experience, by its very nature, is something temporary. This is so obvious that it escaped recognition. There was the belief that there should be, or would be, an attainment of some kind that would represent the 'end of the journey,' and that such an attainment would still belong to an 'I' that would be changed or enhanced by the attainment.

The idea that spirituality has something to do with specific states, or even emphatic or altered states, is often put forward. Such states can indeed be experienced during or after certain processes and can be the result of intense emotional release processes. The latter may bring the feeling of a 'high' that can be interpreted in terms of brain chemistry and can be quite addictive. It is possible for such a state to be chased after, especially when there is the misunderstanding that it is a sign of drawing closer to the divine as is sometimes advertised by some groups.

An energetic 'high,' a state of deep peace, or a feeling of a mystical love, always goes away! Such compelling states can just as easily be used to adorn the 'I.' If someone has experienced them, it is easy to consider him or herself more divine, closer to God, or special, or better, or holier as a result of having had the experience. Instead of asking for such states, or looking for an enlightenment 'experience,' it is possible to ask: 'Who or what is there when all experiences have ceased? Who or what is there before any experience happened?'

No Liberated 'Me' in Sight

Over the years, after my Eastern excursions, the 'I' trap remained. As with many friends and fellow travelers, there had been much inner work. We had become acquainted with the word 'moksha'—liberation, but this liberation remained elusive. I remained sold on the 'I' idea, the idea that something needed to happen within the frame of the 'I', something that would forever change it. Instead, the ups and downs just kept happening, and if 'nothing' happened over a long stretch of time, I liked it even less.

Sometimes there would be subtle and delightful inner qualities, but it was as if after each climb, the fall came even harder.

Eckhart Tolle speaks of the painbody as an almost independent entity[12]; it seemed to behave just thus. The old mind always came back with a vengeance, and it always felt like a familiar repetition of something painful—something that felt restrictive, constrictive, suffocating, and dressed in guilt, sadness, heaviness, and depressing moods. On the other hand, there were also qualities that spontaneously arose and that were helped along by meditation and by being with what is. They had a flavor of freshness, expansiveness, lightness; though fleeting, they seemed uncontaminated by the old mind and beyond it.

Over time, it was increasingly obvious that all states were coming and going, and this became even clearer because of meditation. Yet I continued to sense that there would be a certain something that would be more permanent. I really did not know what it could be—only that it could not possibly relate to anything that was already known.

In my late twenties, after a weekend meditation process, there had been a satori. I call it that although some people define satori in a different way. We started at five in the morning and sat till evening, and at night I went out for a walk. All of a sudden, under that night sky, it was as if something inside popped; there was a recognition of being the witness, the empty screen of awareness and not what arises within it. There was the clear insight that 'what I am' had never been touched or affected by anything I had gone through, done, or felt. This awareness was accompanied by an intense joy, a kind which I had never experienced before, because it was not the result of a particular circumstance. It was not lost on me that there was a significance in this 'opening' that had to do with the 'who am I' question. I experienced it as a deep shift, and 'something' was never the same as before.

But, there was still a long journey ahead. Even though I knew I was the watcher, there was still an 'I,' as in, 'I who is witnessing.' In addition, what was being witnessed were still the struggles of a seemingly autonomous 'me as a person' with plenty of feelings of unworthiness and a profound sense of lack, as well as a lack of self-esteem from comparing myself to and needing from seemingly autonomous 'others.'

Trapped in the 'I'

There was still a pervasive sense of being incomplete, perhaps now even more so since lofty spiritual ideals had become part of my world. A search for 'something' continued, but after a few years, it felt as if I was not getting anywhere.

I found myself not sufficiently transformed and integrated, and coming up against the same issues again and again. A popular suggestion that I heard hundreds of times was to 'go deeper, be more watchful.' Increasingly, this sounded hollow. The statement suggests, not only that something should be done, but that 'something' would be found in the depth. But where was that depth and how deep was that depth relative to a lesser depth? Watchfulness was not enough, and should be greater, but is it a thing that can be measured? And is there someone who can even be watchful, is watchfulness even within one's control? Very subtly, the prescription pointed to a 'somewhere else' and 'a future point in time,' and away from what is. It reinforced the conundrum by implying that 'what is, is incomplete and not ok', and what one does is not enough, while simultaneously enhancing that incompleteness by adding another layer to it.

Over the course of years, I became worn out by the inner search. I wanted a 'regular' life in which the priority of inner work took a back seat to paid work. The notion of 'stillness' had never held a particular attraction for me, and meditation as the main focus was disappearing, but not without a pinch of guilt about concerning myself more with mundane life. By moving on to other horizons, the longing to find access to a spiritual fulfilment faded, and yet, deep down, forgetting all about it while consciously not paying attention to it was never quite possible either.

The 'I' Idea at the Root of Conditioning

There is a common understanding that liberation is the result of 'working through our conditioning' and that this is required. At the time, I understood conditioning as the cause of the specific make up of the body-mind—that whatever happened when we grew up shaped the way we were.

Today I would say that conditioning is mainly the process through which we become identified with the particular elements of the evolving body-mind. We all learn early on that there is an 'I,' first as a result of a physical boundary with another who is 'out there' and occupies a different area of space than 'me.' Our 'I's subsequently accept qualities given by the outside—being a boy or a girl; pretty or cute; smart, quiet, or rambunctious—and latch onto them. Feelings are also discovered; they are ours, or theirs. Perceived character traits give the 'I' further definition—'I am this and that but not those other things.' The whole psycho-physical system undergoes development, and whether unpleasant things like blocked emotions happen as a result of it or not, that emotional-mental-physical-spiritual system is conceived as 'us.' We identify with its story and construct our identity around its perceived qualities of good and bad, desirable and undesirable.

Because the body-mind is a time-based organism, complete with a memory record in which all kinds of 'old stuff' is stored, the 'I' is believed to be the result of what happened in the past. In other words, it is believed to be the result of conditioning—the effect of a number of causes that lie in the past (genetic, karmic, life history, collective history). Because the 'I' is then experienced as limiting, one tries to get out or change some of its qualities by trying to undo its history which is by then, only memory. We try to decondition ourselves by working backwards through the accumulated past via memory. This can be done to better understand how this particular body-mind of ours has been shaped, or as a reaction to a painful condition that begs resolution. There are a number of psychological methods available at this level. But by reshaping the supposed 'I,' the tradition of the 'I' as a latch for qualities is continued. That 'I' now becomes an 'I' that works through 'conditioning' in order to become free.

This is a self-defeating proposition, and it was one particular lesson that had to be repeated many times; expending a great deal of effort, money, and time on it. In society, everyone is believed to have an 'I.' This assumption is mostly unchallenged since everything that happens is somehow understood to refer to an entity called 'I.'

While I imagined liberation to mean the 'me' would be free, now I would say that the body-mind process—something which happens within the realm of time-based appearance—is freed from the 'me' idea. The body, its mind, and all else which appears, simply go on. It is quite liberating to have no 'I' idea attached to them.

5

Awareness — The Beginning, the Middle, and the End

A few natural mechanisms such as laughing, orgasm, sneezing, and dreamless sleep take us out of the 'I.' This is because in such moments, the organism is not able sustain the dual thought-subject and its corresponding other-object. However the effects are short-lived. Within the attempt to bring about the same effect in a lasting manner, awareness is an important key — a special, almost alchemical ingredient. Prayer is another such key, one that belongs to a path centered around love, devotion, and the heart, for example as practiced among the Sufis. Whichever approach one prefers does not matter.

Awareness and What it Reflects

Awareness does not need to be created; it is already there. When looking at it more closely and trying to find out what it does, we usually think of it in terms of 'being aware of something' and then noticing that awareness of something being quickly followed by an awareness of some other thing. When we look at what we are aware of, we find there is a seemingly endless succession of phenomena that is constantly arising and subsiding; what is perceived changes all the time.

We speak of being conscious of things only when they appear in the light of awareness. So how can we know that there is indeed an awareness that is different from its content? Is there such a thing or is it an inference—if 'consciousness of something' is there, awareness must be there too? In the context of spirituality, awareness is a big deal, but why and what is it?

Awareness is special because it is not only something we have, but what we are. If one is attentive, one finds that there is an unchanging quality of awareness in which the changing world appears, an awareness that is never affected by the ever-changing content. To a certain extent, everyone already knows this quality of awareness. People who are beyond middle age sometimes say that inside they feel as they did when they were young, even though the body has acquired wrinkles, is forgetful, and cannot move very fast anymore.

In spiritual circles, sometimes people assume they should be aware of more than they presently are. I have heard this especially from people influenced by Buddhism who feel they should be more aware of the suffering of the world. If there is a sense in which awareness really is like the mirror, the open sky, the limitless background on which everything else appears, how could one have more or less of it? The manifest phenomena that appear against this background appear as one's world. Even when the appearances include thoughts that there should be different content or more content—I feel my big toe but I should feel my hair growing as well if I was totally aware—one still remains the watcher.

The critical question is 'Who am I?' not 'What is appearing for me?' Attention can be directed, for example towards a flower, and can involve spending much time looking at its details, getting lost in it. Awareness is what includes such a focusing of attention as well as fast action in other circumstances. Awareness is what's always aware; it does not choose and does not sleep.

Awareness Seduced by Phenomena

That which keeps appearing, the constant coming and going of an endless kaleidoscope of phenomena, is one's world. Because this world appears as forms, one can make distinctions within those phenomena and apply descriptions. It is the relative that can be described not the absolute. A form is only perceivable when it has differentiated itself from the background, the background does not have form. The old Chinese symbol for differentiation into form is the yin and yang. Eve eating the apple of knowledge also indicates the ability to differentiate.

When we pay attention to what is, we perceive all kinds of differentiated phenomena. They appear as something other than the 'noticing quality' of awareness itself. It is not so easy to notice the noticing capacity of awareness because the content is usually in the foreground. In other words, it is not easy to see where awareness ends and its content starts. One way of explaining this conundrum, in a metaphorical way, is that all phenomena have the ability to capture, almost seduce our attention as it is attracted by the perceived object. We get caught up in the perceived and forget about the perceiving quality itself, whether that perception is via the five senses or through an inner capability.[13] For example, when watching television, we lose ourselves in the content and forget the watcher.

I remember hearing a saying that 'God is in love with his creation.' I see a parallel with awareness—any kind of perceived phenomenon has an intriguing, almost hypnotizing, effect. One could say that objects put consciousness in a state of trance.

This tendency is at work when we pay attention to what is in the moment. Whatever appears has already caught one's attention even if it is something painful. If there is a memory that produces a pang of pain or if one finds oneself in conflicted feelings, awareness does not automatically shy away from it. Everyone has noticed that 'negative' content attracts and holds attention just like any other content. Awareness does not choose its object, the object has already drawn attention to itself once there is awareness of it. Attention comes from the Latin *attendere*, meaning to stretch toward — attention stretches towards any object. Attention loses itself in perceiving forms almost like the primordial consciousness diffuses itself into the multitude of material forms.

How can awareness be the path if recognition of self comes about by being aware of whatever is perceived in the moment since whatever is perceived is an object? When there is always something showing up, an endless succession of one thing after another, even if they come from deep inner worlds, how can this lead to liberation?

Whenever awareness is considered, there is a duality at work — awareness and whatever is being reckoned; so how can awareness be a path to oneness? The difficulty for the 'seeker' is that if he or she follows the logic of being present in the moment, all he or she is now aware of are a multitude of objects (perceptions). There may be a thoughtless state, or stillness, but it is still appearing to a perceiving agent as a perceived object.

By turning away from the perceived content, or letting it all just pass through, or turning inside to where this awareness originates, it is possible for one to realize 'I am this awareness.' Awareness 'stretches back' toward itself instead of the perceived form. Because of the seductive quality of forms, this is not so easy. When awareness turns upon itself, or falls back into itself, it is formless consciousness knowing itself directly. This is not a philosophical equation; it is like being the very light before anything, including time and space, have sprung from it.

The Ongoing Trance

In some contexts, trance refers to a paranormal state brought about by certain preparatory rituals practiced especially by indigenous people around the world.

But there is also an everyday trance which is not paranormal but very common; a kind of sleep-state—a persisting absorption with the elements of one's world. Gurdjieff highlighted this condition and his movement techniques[14] were geared towards developing a more acute awareness in order to break the sleep-like state. NLP[15] is a mind technology that is also based on the observation that most people are in a trance, but contrary to Gurdjieff, its goal is not alertness but rather pleasant altered states and behavioral change. NLP wants to change the quality of the trance from unpleasant to pleasant, but does not concern itself with breaking the trance, and it uses hypnotic methods for this purpose.

I am using the term trance to highlight the fact that any 'thing' can draw attention to itself and absorb it—from mundane things like soap suds when washing dishes to a memory of the past; from feelings to thoughts. When attentiveness is thus turned towards an object, there is usually a simultaneous self-forgetting, a forgetting of the one who is aware of it all. This also happens when the object is a story, especially one's own life story.

At some point I asked myself why it is so evidently difficult to break the enthralment of the belief of being 'me and my story'; to be aware of the spell that it casts and to come to know that one is not the story. Some people may say there is no one to be aware, no one there to break the spell, and yet, not everyone can say this with first hand insight. It may be repeated as a kind of new dogma, a learned conviction. Similarly, in today's parlance, sometimes it is heard that it is seen by no one that there is no one in the story. But if it is seen, there must be a something which is seeing it.

Anything can capture our attention, put us under a bit of a spell, especially our own life stories. Life stories can be breathtaking tragedies or comedies or a mixture of both; they have a validity of their own. Most literature is inspired by them. What I am trying to question here is not the validity of the story, but rather the tendency to mistake the moving picture for the screen, so to speak. If one pays for a movie, one does not want to look at an empty screen. What is compelling is the story, and as attention is drawn to the symphony of pictures, sounds and events, it is any kind of action that allows one to forget one is the watcher. As a result, awareness hides itself within the dynamic web of phenomenal appearance.

I also wondered why it is so difficult to question the concepts that underlie certain growth groups. When asked to look at the specific implications of some of those concepts, I found that people often respond by saying 'Why, so many things happened for me in the group.' Getting drawn into the story can even occur within meditation processes, and a great deal more within psychological processes. When there is additional drama, exciting events, or compelling states, it is like going from black and white television to color TV: the story intensifies. There is a great deal more intensity than in daily life — something is happening. Since one is already entranced by the life story, the additional intrigue makes it more captivating. It becomes a better movie from which it is even more difficult to extricate oneself, or rather remember oneself.

Distinctions within the Content of Awareness

Because forms are distinct, when paying attention to what arises within awareness, it is possible to differentiate between levels, or layers, of phenomena, such as those pertaining to the body, to emotions, to mental and intuitive functioning. It may then be noticed that these layers of the functioning of the body-mind system are interwoven. In the chakra system, the layers are called bodies and are assigned to a particular chakra (energy center). Each body or layer is seen as steering a particular set of functions. Whatever one calls them, layers, bodies, or subtle energies, they permeate and influence each other, and this can be observed.

To give a few examples — emotions affect the physical body (anger results in clenched teeth, for example); thoughts such as 'he does not love me' may bring sadness; reading financial headlines may evoke fear; a dream may result in solving a theoretical scientific question, such as in the famous example of Mr. Kekule, a chemist, who dreamt of a snake biting its tail and thereby knew the structure of the benzene molecule to be a ring. All these different levels are interrelated through a complex web of memory, life experience, personality structure, genetic disposition and other factors.

The intention here is not to provide models for how this inter-relation works in detail, but rather to simply state the general fact. There are some spiritual approaches that mainly concern themselves with the level of thought, with how the thought process functions, and which tend to postulate that everything is thought and that 'thought creates emotion.' There are, however, situations in which emotion arises as a reaction, not to thought, but to an occurrence. If someone steps on your foot in a subway, most probably there is a shade of anger as the fight or flight response of the body kicks in. Also, emotions have a certain vibrational quality. Our emotional bodies respond to frequencies in the surroundings. For example, if there is a lot of anger in a room, even if it is unexpressed, it will trigger this emotion in others. This is not a reaction to thought. The postulate that everything is a thought or a concept is itself a thought. Awareness notices this postulation as well as other phenomena that are beyond thought and the mental level.

The Intuitive Layer of the Body-Mind

Most people are aware of a body, emotions, and thinking, but intuitive abilities appear a bit more mysterious although they function in daily life. They are referred to here only as one example of the more subtle layer of the body-mind.

Beyond the mental level is the layer of intuitive knowing and creative imagination. This is the layer where a problem solving 'good' idea can pop into one's mind seemingly out of nowhere; where one can have a dream about something which then happens later on in the future. It is where precognition happens, where we 'pick up' information about a person, place, or situation. In this dimension the world becomes more subjective and sometimes unverifiable by another, such as in the case of someone seeing auras, colors, or energies.[16]

There are people, so-called realists, who dispute everything they can't see or touch, but everyone has had experiences which indicate that the physical realm is not the only mode of existence. A lot of people have had the experience of thinking of a particular person just seconds before that person called on the phone. Another example is of people commenting that a certain person has a certain 'glow' about them. These subtle phenomena occur and are perceived by many people, though mostly in rudimentary form. They have not been valued much in the rational scientific age and are often even suppressed in children, even though in other cultures they are cherished. Sometimes phenomena of a psychic nature happen to otherwise 'normal' people in unforeseen and spontaneous ways. When they do, it is good to have some kind of frame of reference of what they constitute.[17]

Some people have psychic abilities. These are a function of the intuitive layer of the body-mind, just as the gift of artistic imagination is a function of this layer. In self-discovery groups, there are sometimes exercises during which all participants walk through the room and then spontaneously tell the persons they meet what they see about them. Sometimes such brief statements can mirror a part of the other person's reality to a surprising degree; this is also a function of intuition. Sometimes though, such intuitive seeing is interspersed with projection—a muddling of the perception of what is one's own reality and what belongs to the other. It is good to clarify what projection is before the exercise. Because there is quite a large margin of error, this intuitive ability should be used with great care or it can easily turn into a power trip, for example when one person feels that his or her 'psychic impressions' are necessarily an adequate description of another person's reality.

Perceptions that pertain to our own physical bodies may include an awareness of a tense shoulder muscle, tension around the diaphragm, or a pain in the knee. But there are also intuitive phenomena such as heat sensations, a sense that certain areas of the body seem more dense or that they seem to be filled with a grey fog. One may perceive that there is a field around the body that extends beyond the physical and that there is a vibration within it or maybe a 'knot' or a streaming sensation. Certain areas of the body may be perceived as filled with a certain color, or even bright light. These are all examples of being aware of the subtle energetic qualities within oneself. The word energy is used because such phenomena are not of a dense material nature. Another example of this level is found in acupuncture; anyone who has experienced it has probably had a perception of an 'energy flow.'

Being in awareness means letting anything that arises, including perceptions of the subtle layers, be there without pushing them away, without denying them or striving to have something particular happen. Some people have more astute subtle perceptions than others; we are not all made the same way. Sometimes someone identifies with this aspect of their functioning and then says 'I am psychic.' While this can simply be descriptive, it can also signify an identification with such abilities, and that they are being made into an attribute of the persona. This can go as far as believing 'I am spiritual because I have intuition,' or that 'being psychic is spiritual.'

6

Inner Work

Is There Spiritual Growth?

'Going inside,' 'meditating,' 'being in the now,' 'being aware of all that is' brings the inner functioning of ever subtler layers into focus. What is likely to be discovered is that on every level, a positive experience has its own kind of shadow. A sense of feeling secure can be quickly followed by anxiety, satisfaction by frustration, power by helplessness, an expanded heart state by painful disconnectedness, and clarity by a sense that everything is in a fog. Even a mystical transcendent experience can turn into existential despair.[18] On the other hand, every darkness, when explored, can morph into a very distinct luminescent opening. It appears that as one thing is being worked through, another level is reached and then followed by a falling back—again and again. The idea of spiritual growth implies that there is some kind of solidifying of experience on ever higher levels. This comes from the hope that peak experiences mean progress. But after such heights, all too often, one comes tumbling or crashing down.

The idea of spiritual growth is widely accepted. If it does not work in a linear way, then at least in a spiral, but upward is the direction it is supposed to go. This makes sense however, only from the perspective of the 'I' that believes itself to be a continuum in time and that it is defined by experiences it identifies as 'mine.' The 'I' is invested in the growth idea while tending to blind itself to the 'down' that follows the 'up.' But if the notion of time falls away, the idea of growth falls away as well, and if there is no 'I,' experiences are liberated from having to fit into the growth idea—a mutual liberation. This does not mean that within the phenomenal there are no more changes or happenings, only that attachment to those changes has ceased.

When the idea of growth falls away, the attachment to the idea that one should be in congruency with one's imagined preferred quality of 'spiritual progress' also falls away. If there is no need to be any other way than the way one is, guilt and pretense cannot catch hold. One can be more restful because there is no need to get anywhere 'spiritually.' It becomes much easier to accept life as it presents itself and to let oneself be carried by its current.

Exploring Meditation

When speaking about meditation, it should first be noted that it is an idea and that everyone understands it somewhat differently. Its understanding is shaped by tradition, by others, and by one's own exposure to it or lack thereof. Generally, it refers to either something that happens 'within,' in the inner realm, or to a formal process to which a person submits in order to make spiritual progress.

The idea of meditation as something that furthers spiritual growth gives it a particular place in the context of spirituality—an activity that is rather a non-activity. In its essence, meditation is about discovering awareness, about how awareness reflects all content without being touched by it and coming to know this awareness as inescapable and already there.

Meditation is watching whatever arises in one's consciousness without any preferences and judgments about the content—including not judging the judgments—and gradually becoming aware of the watching capacity itself.

The innate faculty of watching, or awareness, does not think or do or move, but is rather aware of thinking, doing, moving. It is not about having or looking for great 'meditative' experiences even though they can and probably will happen along the way, just as much as difficult experiences will happen along the way. To watch means being receptive, noticing, being open to what appears. It is sometimes referred to as 'pure listening' or 'pure seeing,' although this is not done with the physical ears or eyes; such words are references to the awareness of being aware.[19]

Meditation is not about becoming a 'seasoned meditator' or believing that doing formal meditation is superior to other activities. It is about becoming acquainted with the faculty of witnessing whatever is appearing within one's consciousness, an awareness that itself is never touched by the arising content. If anything else, meditation is meant to discover this.

No Instant Gratification

In this day and age, meditation is hailed as a stress relief and relaxation activity. Even Western doctors recommend it now as a method of preventing stress-related disease. Although it is often equated to 'sitting silently,' it is not that easy. Whoever has tried to sit silently on a meditation pillow in front of the Buddha statue has probably realized that peace and quiet are not immediately forthcoming, that one is rather likely to find turmoil instead. When awareness is shed on that which is, tensions in the body, conflicted emotions, and runaway thoughts can come into focus in uncomfortable ways. Meditation will expose defense mechanisms, bring suppressed feelings to the surface, or expose a sense of inner hollowness. Everyone carries more pain than we want to look at; that pain will surface when not pushed away. Watching will make you see what you prefer not to look at. Awareness has a keen way of making one aware of things.

In his series of talks titled "Psychology of the Esoteric," Osho says that people come to him and report that they actually experience increased tensions since they have started meditating. He explains that this is so because meditation brings out all accumulated desires and confusions. This has been my experience as well. In longer meditation processes there were often stretches when there was a great level of inner torment, seemingly out of nowhere and unprovoked by any current situation. By moving through such phases, most often, surprising and sudden openings into harmonic well-being or a sense of lightness unfolded.

Meditation is not about an outcome, it is about being with whatever is, from one breath to the next. It is not a goal-oriented activity. It is a mistaken belief that meditation is about obliterating the thought process (which is impossible) or that it will bring instant relaxation. Sometimes, people go into meditation with a program of what they would like to find, and if they are influenced by Zen, this may include the idea that it is important to hear chirping birds. Meditation should be about letting oneself be there as one is, getting to know oneself exactly as one is, from the inside, and forgetting any kind of outcome. After all, it cannot produce that which precedes it—beingness itself.

Meditation Techniques

Techniques can be helpful in becoming aware of the watching faculty, even though the latter is not confined to sitting on a pillow or being in a group retreat. The watching faculty is there 24/7—consciousness never sleeps. Formal meditation helps to discover it, while committing to a structured group process helps one experiment with it and explore it. In a group, the collective effort makes it easier to adhere to a structured schedule, to relax into it and flow with it, to see what happens when distractions of daily life are eliminated for some time. An outer structure helps one get away from habitual response patterns that rule the normal daily activity. Not everyone is drawn to the notion of meditation though, especially when it is equated to silent sitting. This does not seem very attractive for the outgoing A-type personality for whom meditation is considered especially beneficial from a health point of view.

Nowadays, one can experiment with a number of meditation techniques that include body movement, an approach that is somewhat easier for our famously restless minds than just sitting for days. Yoga is a popular form of this approach, although many people practice it predominantly for its physical benefits. My favorite meditation of all times was darkness meditation. In the early morning, we would sit for an hour in a darkroom that was outfitted so no single ray of light could penetrate. We would sit there looking into the darkness with wide open eyes, losing any sense of time.

One other technique I found very effective is the "Enlightenment Intensive" that was invented some time in the 70s. It is a very useful process for beginners. The very structured process makes use of communication, and because of the way this communicative element is integrated, it allows one to pierce layers of self like an arrow, guided by the question 'tell me who you are.' Since the 'who am I' question is asked by a partner, it is a great help in staying focused. By responding immediately according to whatever is in one's consciousness at that very moment, there is more directness and less danger of spacing out compared to a silent meditation process.

Examples of meditations that are more challengingly structured are Vipassana and Zazen, and they require a certain level of commitment. They usually last at least a week, with the sitting starting early in the morning and continuing into the night. In Vipassana, the focus of attention is on the breath. Breathing is an automatic body mechanism that we are normally not conscious of, but its ongoing rhythm provides a certain constant and has a grounding effect. By watching the breath, awareness easily centers around the physical navel center, the hara. In ZaZen, one sits looking at a white wall, something that has a relaxing effect on the physical eye. The white wall literally functions as a metaphor for the empty screen of awareness.

Pursuing meditation depends on personality preferences, the phase of life one finds oneself in, and whether one is drawn to structured meditation or not. It may be what life has to offer at some point, but if there is no resonance with it, one will probably not sign up. If one does, it must be assumed that it is exactly the right move at that point in time. But traditional meditation is only one form of inner investigation, treasured in other times that were not as fast-paced as our own. I remember, for example, Yogananda stating that he spent hours meditating in a temple as a teenager; for today's teenagers, this kind of pastime would seem rather odd.

Many people got acquainted with meditation through Zen after it was embraced by contemporary Western culture a few decades ago. Around the same time that increasing numbers of Westerners were going to India in search of spirituality, they also went to Japan and imported Zen, complete with its vocabulary, rituals, and particular tenets. Zen thrived hundreds of years ago in rural Japan, and within its tradition, 'direct experience' is a favored approach, either by sitting in meditation or by performing daily living tasks.

When mentioning Zen, it is necessary to mention its beliefs since those beliefs somewhat belie its perceived simplicity. For example, even in the Western adaptation of Zen, there is a belief in dharma transmission by which the enlightenment of a successor is certified by a teacher (roshi). This certification is mostly a political strategy of ensuring the continuance of the organization. The power within the organization of the temple or center is derived from the accepted dogma of a lineage, by which a mysterious buddha substance that originates in Buddha himself is transmitted. Here, the understanding that Zen is about simplicity is contradicted because the lineage theory perpetuates 'true nature' as something elusive, mysterious, and attainable only by a few. Zen also advances the 'attainment in stages' myth where such attainment is considered the result of years of not only meditation, but also seniority within the hierarchical structure of the Zen temple or center.

The idea of formal meditation can be a serious and heavy one if it is felt that one 'should lead a life of meditation' or be an earnest practitioner, and that without it, no spiritual 'progress' would be made. A technique will not lead to realization in a linear fashion. It can at best help dismantle a host of misconceptions and speed up the process of getting existentially exasperated with the paradox of seeking that which already is. At worst, a technique will keep us in the loop of hoping for some attainment. I was at times not free of feeling guilt about not meditating enough, but in hindsight, every action was perfectly appropriate. There were times when a daily meditation was important for me and many others when it felt dry and unappealing. Other times I was consumed with grief, restlessness, or upset and the last thing I would want to do was any kind of meditation.

When undergoing a meditation process, I found it most useful to simply and consistently stay with whatever arose. Just following what happened from moment to moment with a heightened alertness was intriguing in its own right. It was my preference to not have this process clouded by preconceived ideas. Maybe because of this, I was never drawn towards meditation in a neo-Buddhist environment. I wanted to stay with what was happening and did not like to have it filtered by preconceived ideas. I looked at exactly what was happening with the next breath instead of looking at the experience against the backdrop of concepts such as desirelessness, compassion, suffering, or even buddha nature.

Whatever form of meditation is embarked on, it could be said that the inner being brings a person to meditation because it wants to make itself known. Consciousness which has hidden itself in the many forms that are at the same time its expression, strives to know itself. Perhaps all meditation and seeking can be seen as facets of this impersonal game of consciousness. It is consciousness which says 'come looking for me.' This is felt as a thirst, a hunger, an echo of remembrance of being that same consciousness. And as long as the 'thou art that' is not recognized, the game of searching continues, in meditation, or in another form.

Dialectic between Meditation and Psychological Methods

For Zen and similar meditation approaches, the prescription is to just sit, but the practice of just sitting and the simple attitude of mindfulness are not easily accessible to the Western body and psyche. We suffer the effects of sensory overload and when we try to be in a quiet state of mind and body, an inherent restlessness always bubbles up to the surface. We also live in a culture that favors doing, achievement, and self-importance. As a result, budding attempts at 'just being' all too often flush compulsive thinking, physical agitation, and emotional irritability to the forefront.

While meditation can give the impression that an issue that was struggled with evaporates just by watching, observing, and alertness, it is likely that one comes up against certain inner knots time and again. Such a knot may be accompanied by a continued sense of inner, and sometimes physically felt, heaviness. Such a condition makes any silent meditation a painful if not impossible chore. Watching loosens inner control mechanisms so that emotional content that was hidden can sometimes suddenly arise in the form of old painful memories or traumas. Emotional tensions make it difficult to just watch because the inner space then feels anything but spacious.

In our modern psyches, we are often conflicted, and often, it is our awareness of exactly such conflicted-ness that initiates the 'who am I' question or the 'search.' Everyone experiences aspects of this conflict: wanting love while rejecting it; needing from the other and being afraid of losing independence; enjoying oneself and feeling guilty for it. To avoid the conflicted-ness because either we have read scriptures which say those conflicts are not real, or because they should not happen for an advanced meditator, is self-deception.

It makes sense for therapeutic settings to be sought out when strong emotions are present and to then move through the feelings by exploring them using psychological methods. Perhaps people who have never accorded how sad they truly are can share the depth of their feeling with others. It may be exactly by attending to it that some energy which had not been allowed expression can surface. Perhaps certain emotions had been avoided, and realizing that these are nevertheless present in a suppressed form, someone may want to acknowledge them by addressing them with the help of a therapist or a therapeutic group that allows this kind of open exploration.

Certain spiritual traditions or purely meditational methods have said to not involve emotional work. It is my sense that the tradition of placing them under prohibition lingers on in such contexts. What comes into awareness as 'us' as we turn inside is probably emotional content—we experience ourselves as being it. Jean Klein, for example, points out that "what surfaces during meditation are residues of the past," and that these residues appear as "localized energy."[20] He was talking about a physical tension in this case, but we also locate ourselves around emotional tension. It is how we perceive ourselves or how we are for ourselves. Psychological approaches are needed because emotional work is part of inner work, especially when the immediate experience is of an emotional nature. Psychological explorations are just another way of being aware of what is.

How someone deals with one's inner being may differ according to one's personality, and for some, neither emotional nor meditative methods are an option. But choosing one approach over the other also depends on discerning what is happening in the present context. Just because a meditation process was the thing to do yesterday does not necessarily make it the best choice today.

The "Diamond Work" of H. A. Almaas is an example of a synthesis between the two poles of the dialectic. He says that "in traditional spiritual teachings, there has been some kind of rejection or disdain for psychological work. Many teachers actually say not to do psychological work—it's a waste of time, or a distraction. A deeper understanding is that spiritual work includes psychology."[21] In his work, the ego is not seen as something to be gotten rid of. Instead, it is investigated *as* the particular dynamic in which we function; it shapes perception and inner states, and exactly within and through this functioning, subtler realms of spirituality arise.

The potentials of this kind of synthesis is also described in an interesting article by John J. Prendergast, specifically, the possible role of psychotherapy within the context of non-dual awareness.[22] He says that if a psychotherapist has an understanding of the latter, it will impact his or her work because the "awakening of nondual awareness also facilitates the depth and transformative power of inquiry.... Discernment is significantly enhanced. As therapists learn to live in the unknown, increasingly free of conclusions, they are better able to assist their clients to do the same. They see thoughts for what they are—just thoughts.... They know the peace and freedom of living without attachment to any story of how things are or should be. This is especially the case with the story of being a separate self, which is unquestioned by all conventional psychotherapies."[23] Consequently, psychotherapy is allowed to 'rest in unknowing.' This unknowing is the alpha and omega of meditation—seeing what is without judgement, freely resting in awareness itself.

Meditation as a Natural Ability

Is it possible to refrain from adopting particular attitudes about meditation? Some consider meditation a higher or better activity because it is said to lead to liberation. Others claim it will not lead out of illusion. In our society, with its preference for ego-based activity, it is quite often considered a bad use of one's limited time. Can we say that meditation is like everything else, that it comes and goes when the time and the conditions are appropriate, and that everyone has at least a taste of it when walking, gardening, working, or playing sports? Is there actually anything which is not meditation?

Attitudes about meditation are plentiful, and often they are loaded with shoulds and should nots, for example, when, where, how, with whom, and in what setting meditation should be done. There are ideas about what meditative persons look like or how they walk, such as slowly, with mindfulness. Some people conceive of meditation as an activity of the 'I,' and therefore strive to be good and consistent meditators. 'Being a meditator' is then just another label attached to the 'I' idea, possibly giving it a flavor of being superior, and even creating stress from trying to live up to the 'good meditator' image.

Alertness as an Antidote to 'I'-Identification

When one is walking, just being with the movement, the sensation of sunlight on the face, the sound of the wind, the smells of the earth—the thought process may disappear for a while and a natural sense of just being may appear. But turning inside while having the eyes closed and the body in a sitting position brings more focus to the inner world, because one can leave any concern with the outer environment behind for awhile. Reliance on the senses is suspended for some time. One does not have to look to see where one is putting the foot for the next step.

Some people are never drawn to turning inside in this manner, which requires a certain focus. It depends on the individual's makeup. For example, traditional Yoga acknowledges such differences by defining karma yoga as being for those whose path consists of engagement with the outer world, bhakti yoga for those who are inclined towards religious devotion and service, and for those who have a natural inclination towards discovering inner functioning, jnana yoga, or focused meditation.

While awareness—which to me is never a state but the light in which states appear and disappear—is always functioning no matter what the 'path' is, in meditation there is an added quality of alertness, or in other words, a conscious act of staying alert. While being alert and attentive towards what is going on inside, it is usually noticed that whatever is appearing is constantly changing.

Today, there seems to be almost a backlash against meditation, often coming from recent Neo-Advaita doctrines. It may be wondered if there is an underlying disappointment, because one could not control one's spiritual progress, or own awakening, through meditation. The pendulum seems to swing between two poles. One pole consists of a belief that ever more must be watched, that there are ever more unconscious patterns needing to be dragged into the light, and that one's chance at enlightenment is the effect of 'clocking in' enough meditation hours. Representative of the other pole is an attitude for which all practice is illusory, and which often meets the question of meditation with a shrug of the shoulder, and discards any practice because it does not deliver the desired results. Of course, meditative practice cannot create that which precedes it, it arises out of beingness just like everything else arises out of it. But if it is discovered that there was never anyone who 'practiced', it follows that there is no one 'not' to practice. And when critiquing practice, who is there to take a stand, either for or against it? Coincidentally, by favoring satsangs over meditative practice, I wonder if it is implied that they can bring results better or faster.

It may be worthwhile to free meditative practice from the hope for an outcome, and thus eliminate some of the weighty expectations which are often put upon it. If the critique assumes that meditation necessarily tries to establish permanent inner states of a higher order, at least in my experience and precisely because of meditation, it was obvious how all states were coming and going. Yet I continued to sense that there would be a certain something that would be more permanent. I really did not know what it could be—only that it could not possibly relate to anything that was already known.

I remember when I came across the Vigyan Bhairav Tantra which is Sanskrit for 'Techniques for Going Beyond Consciousness.' It is a text said to be five thousand years old. In it, Shiva's lover poses a question about the nature of life, and as an answer, Shiva gives short descriptions of 112 meditation techniques. The text indicates that everyone, no matter which path they prefer or in which culture they live, will find a technique amongst the 112 suitable for them. Osho talks about the Vigyan Bhairav Tantra in his *Book of Secrets* and says that "Basically, this is the source book for all techniques which are known all over the world."[24]

When I reviewed the techniques, I found one which looked appealing and made me want to try it. It stated: "Whenever in-breath and out-breath fuse, at this instant touch the energy-less, energy-filled center." I discovered that at that point, nothing is happening at all—no inner lights exploding—just nothing. At the time, I still expected enlightenment to be a grand event, and the insight that arose from this meditation technique did away with this idea. Trying to capture the turnaround point of the breath is like finding the highest point of a sine wave, where the ascending branch turns into the descending branch. This point is so infinitesimally small that it does not occupy any space, there is no movement whatsoever. It basically falls outside of spatial reference and outside of time; it is complete stillness, in other words, there is no space for any differentiation between an 'I' and what is.

One should not summarily conclude that all meditation is about looking for a state. The preceding example indicates just the contrary. Maybe one way to look at meditation is to see it as the never ending answer to a never ending question. Whatever is being said, here and elsewhere, is an encouragement to keep looking. Self-knowledge, or rather 'no-self-not-knowing,' can never come secondhand, it reveals itself through trial and error.

7

Language and the Thinking Process

As human beings, we are at an evolutionary stage that allows us a more or less sophisticated use of language. Language is the medium in which thinking functions. Despite the fact that language is such a beautiful gift, some spiritual traditions tend to see 'thought' as the big stumbling stone to knowing who one is, the big hindrance in 'seeing things as they are.' But if there is a thinking mode, who will object except the thinker who wants to be a no-thinker, not knowing he can be neither. If one is indeed beyond any thing and any appearance, how could thinking interfere with it?

Language Symbols

A word symbol is a sign with a physical component consisting of a sequence of letters, a corresponding sound, and a reference to an object outside of language, that is, its meaning. Language is the combination of word symbols in a meaningful manner. A word symbol, by definition, is not the thing it refers to, it is an abstraction because it is not the specific thing. Language works because word symbols can be understood to mean a certain thing. Meaning is assigned by social convention, whether implicitly or explicitly by definitions such as in science.

Language is a medium of communication. It does not just name isolated things, it also describes their relationships to each other. Verbs describe the state of an object—which itself is represented by a noun—and its relation to another thing, as in 'the ball hits the basket.' Through our use of language, models of reality are gradually developed: first we observe, then name, then describe how things relate. Describing reality by using sentences also creates a new 'language' reality. If I am not on a basketball court where the 'the ball hits the basket' is an actual happening, but am reading that sentence in a novel, then language has constituted its own reality, a kind of parallel reality that is not the actual reality. Sometimes it is forgotten that words, spoken or thought, are not the thing.

The Thinking Process and the Function of Language

Everyone is somehow aware that there is a certain level of internal verbalizing or 'thinking,' which when watched more closely, is discovered to be somewhat automatic and not always very logical. It seems to go on whether one wants it or not, in a more or less compulsive or random, associative or reflexive manner. Sometimes one cannot stop thinking about something particular, other times thoughts show up and one does not know where they've come from.

One form that the inner process of thinking may take is self-talk, an inner dialogue or animated internalized conversations with imagined others. Once, I observed a very large red full moon rising quickly over a mountain ridge. In the perception of this there were no words, yet I realized how after only a few seconds, I had started telling myself the story of how I sat on the balcony watching this large moon. This kind of storytelling is constantly going on in the thinking process. I talked to someone after a meditation and he said he had incessant inner dialogue with a person who was not there. Who has not done this?

For communication, we need the ability to tell stories within the medium of language; it is an important developmental stage in childhood. But then this activity takes on a life of its own and goes on in the background like a radio. Some people are more identified with this inner verbalizing than others who are generally more aware of their emotional process. Still, most of us have known states where compulsive thinking had taken over and we could not put an end to it. Or perhaps we have experienced 'thinking something' but hardly being aware of what and why.

It can be said that (a) thinking goes on, although one is not always conscious of which thoughts are going on and why, (b) thinking occurs on a level other than the physical because we can see someone walking across a room but cannot see what he or she is thinking, and (c) thinking predominantly goes on in the form of internalized language. Nothing about this is unfamiliar, we all have this in common. It is one mode of our functioning, and like physical processes that happen in time, thinking also happens in time. The thinking process also happens in the material realm, albeit a subtler one than the physical. For example, thinking activity can be detected not only by measuring brain waves, experiments also show that plants are responsive to thoughts.

It is often recommended to people who are meditating to become aware of the gap between thoughts. This is an invitation to simply be aware by staying in the moment because awareness is already beyond thinking. However, this advice can turn into a version of 'don't think of the red elephant' because focusing too much on how thoughts come and go can lead to a tunnel vision where not much else is being noticed. Almost everyone has had a situation of which they could say 'I did not know what to think' or 'I was speechless,' and thus have experienced a non-thinking state. If I don't quite manage to be completely aware of the gap between breaths, can I then conclude it is better to not have a body? If gaps between thoughts are not noticed the way one 'thinks' they should, is it therefore justified to say it is the fault of thinking? Does it mean that the 'intelligence of being' is everywhere else except in the thinking process?

Distorted Concepts of Thinking

Thinking has two components. It is a time-based process and activity; we know that we think. Additionally, there is also a content to thinking that shows up in what we think; it expresses itself in the specific thoughts we are having. Thoughts appear in the form of language and present a mode of storytelling about how we interpret the world and ourselves. They have an implicit meaning which we have adopted through the course of life and constitute what we believe our reality to be.

I have crossed paths with some spiritual approaches that do not seem very fond of 'thought.' For example, I remember once raising a question during a 'meditative inquiry' group session wanting to clarify a certain understanding. Upon hearing the question, someone in the group responded with no reference to its specific content that 'this is just a thought.' But a verbal question always consists of language and is also a 'thought'!

There seem to be two possibilities. One is to simply watch in silence what is going on inside, including the twists and turns the thinking process takes. This of course makes any group inquiry obsolete, it is then really meditation. The second possibility is to engage in verbal communication and investigate the content and meaning of a particular thought in order to question what one assumes to be true or untrue: open inquiry is a verbal undertaking by definition and thus needs a certain verbal acuity to function. The kind of thinking that is worth investigating in this way is likely not just a momentary thought such as 'I need to get the mail,' it is likely to be something we believe, a conviction, an opinion, an idea, or ideology, or concept.

For example, if someone has a 'thought,' that is, an idea, that enlightenment equals celibacy, it is possible to address where this thought came from and how it shapes his or her world view. It can be questioned within the medium of language and this can lead to an opening where the perception of reality is no longer filtered by this particular lens anymore. A thought refers to something outside it, has content, and gives an interpretation. Questioning it is a perfectly good way of dealing with that interpretation.

There is a certain attitude expressed in the phrase 'that's just a thought' that looks at 'thought' as an inferior expression of consciousness. Is thought an obstacle? Does the marvelous ability to use language and think—a functional expression of language—only serve to create technological advances, or poetry, but needs to be restricted or pushed away when it comes to questions about our inner nature? Most importantly, if I don't question the content of 'my' thoughts, ideas, and concepts as they interpret my world, who will?

A corollary example of a somewhat distorted concept of thinking is when distinctions between thought and reality are ignored. If I bump into a piece of furniture, the resulting bruise is not a thought, and spending a morning thinking about skiing is not the same as spending a morning skiing. Postulating that everything is thought may prevent one from engaging reality, and then it can mean that there is one person doing the thinking for everyone else. If no distinctions can be made anymore, because there is a dogma of 'everything is just thought or image', things cannot be properly named and characterized because there is no room nor interest in differentiating between categories of thought.

Sometimes in spiritual circles the goal is said to be a thought-less state, or an 'absence of thoughts.' This is generally 'thought of' as having something to do with truth, enlightenment, presence, etc. Given the twofold nature of thinking, this is mostly understood to be when no thinking is detected in the inner realm. Certainly, thinking can slow down at times, can lose its compulsive nature, while returning when needed for practical usefulness. Dangling the spiritual ideal of a thought-less state cannot possibly mean words cannot be used anymore. In fact, many people who concern themselves greatly with the 'ever limited' nature of thought continue to write and speak profusely.

Since thoughts, in the sense of ideas and opinions, form part of our world, being 'thoughtless' must also mean the web of interpretations which thoughts and ideas represent is penetrated, that this web does not cloud perception anymore, that one is able to see through one's ideas and in this way, the reality behind them is revealed—like a theater curtain going up.

Thought as an Interpretation of Reality

J. Krishnamurti has an impact on the current discussion since he stresses again and again that everything is thought. While I have not been influenced by him, I have read transcripts of talks in which he often repeats that the 'world consists of thought,' and that the 'whole of humanity's past is in thought.' Such statements can become the center of a lofty speculation, and the intent to detect thought as constituting everything, a new holy cow.

Thinking about 'the world as thought' is thinking, and the statement itself is a thought. Whether expressing thought or understanding it, one is functioning on the level of thought, even when claiming that 'all is thought.' This claim is only significant in a spiritual context if meant to catapult one out of a conceptual mode. But, it is thinking trying to turn itself into what lies beyond thought, or the thinker trying to do away with himself by thinking. The intended attempt at spiritual liberation by understanding something as thought while remaining a thinker just does not work. Another way of saying this is that awakening cannot be the result of deduction. Additionally, when putting a lot of emphasis on having to recognize everything as thought, as happens in certain traditions, there is still an 'I' for whom a certain position evidently matters—in this case the position of either believing or propagating the necessity of 'trying to get out from thought'. Thinking or not thinking, what one is remains unaffected, it is prior to every expression and non-expression and thus remains undisturbed by it.

It is may be more fruitful to see how thought interprets reality, and worthwhile to look at the content of the thought material when and where it shows up in concrete ways. For example, thought can take the form of specific beliefs and ready-to-use assumptions about oneself and the world, which in turn, have been shaped by historical processes and collectively shared cultural preferences. One finds oneself believing in ideas that have entered the thought stream by way of the collective in which we live. Those ideas are adopted when they are somehow found useful or necessary to the context. If one does not resonate with a certain political ideology, for example, one will not adopt it. If one resonates with a certain spiritual approach, one will assimilate its ideas.

One of the most widely believed assumptions is of being born, essentially, that one is the body. The body's age is then taken as 'your' age and the body's death, 'your' death. Collective thought comes into one's life in a constant daily stream through society and media in the form of folk wisdom and unquestioned 'opinion' from apparently authoritative sources. It comes in the form of prejudice and everyday myths that may be of a political or economic nature. The different assumptions about God can easily be seen as having been shaped by a specific culture and the way one was exposed to that culture, and thus to be a reflection of the complex history of humanity.

One of the goals of cultural or social studies is to examine how the content of thought (opinion, prejudice, dominant beliefs, social myths, religious beliefs) shapes the sense of reality in cultures and societies. In this text, presumptions which form the backdrop of 'spiritual' understanding are being addressed throughout, and more specifically, the ones I have encountered over time.

For example, with regard to Zen, the concept of dharma transmission can be taken as a reality, while inquiring into it might reveal its nature to be a historically shaped belief. Another example is the concept of 'liberation.' In the past I never questioned it. So many old scriptures and more recent ones talk about it and I just accepted it—believing that liberation is something that can actually be had. The appeal of liberation only makes sense because one feels that one is already unfree, but either notion only makes sense if it refers to an 'I'. The 'I' wants to be the one who possesses liberation, even attempts to 'get' it by leaving itself behind, and that is not possible, as it itself is in the way. Hence, old scriptures point out that even the desire for liberation is already an attachment, or part of the trap.

Another concept that shows up in spiritual circles is of aliveness. I have encountered aliveness equated with being emotionally expressive or seen as a quality that can be acquired or accumulated—something one wants more of. If aliveness is seen as something that one can acquire, a quality, then it comes in ever-changing shades. But fundamentally, it is what one is, even when feeling dreary or bogged down. There may be pleasant states of 'feeling so very alive', but if they are taken as a measure of spiritual progress, one is lost in the realm of phenomena.

'Happiness' or 'bliss' are other notions that usually enter one's thoughts because others speak about them; we hear about divine happiness and compare our situation to what we imagine such happiness to be. We think it is the ultimate candy that one gets to enjoy at the end of the search. If such an idea is adopted and allowed to sink in, one starts waiting for that happiness or bliss, hoping for it. Such hope can create a psychic condition where the 'ideal' of happiness is always missing, always at least an arm's length away. But, again, it is not something to 'get' but what we are.

Perhaps you have come across this phrase: 'If I let go of my mind, a greater intelligence will start functioning.' This is an assumption that greater intelligence is a result of something that I do, something dependent on a cause brought about by 'me.' But this can hardly be so if the 'greater intelligence' is really the uncaused; there can be no 'start' to its functioning. If it is really the transcendent realm, it must always function, whether I am in my mind or not. This is another example of how the belief of needing to do something—in this case 'let go of the mind'—gets planted, and how the interplay between the totality of the whole and its manifestations gets reversed.

Whether one believes or accepts this kind of reasoning, language and thinking are good tools for investigating accepted ideas. In the course of inner investigation, it is always particular and specific beliefs one gets caught in at certain times. But not every idea has the same significance for everyone at the same time, even where they make up the collective discourse and form the reality, or world, of a certain group engaged in spiritual seeking. In the following chapters, a few of the specific ideas that are currently in circulation in spiritual communities are looked at more closely.

8

Models of Reality

Behind any scientific inquiry is a curiosity that asks 'What is this, and why is it so?' The next step asks, 'How is this knowledge useful and what can be gained from it?' Here, one primary feature of the mind shows up as utilitarian; it has influenced how knowledge was and is being acquired. When it comes to knowledge, no one starts at zero. Knowledge builds on all that has come before because all theories, including psychological ones, are informed by preceding ones. Their concepts form models of reality.

Scientific Models of Reality

Science looks at empirical data and strives to find connections and causalities among them. In the scientific process, a hypothesis is postulated and then verified or discarded according to the results of the experimental observation of objective data. Newton observed an apple falling from the tree, experimented with falling objects and postulated the theorem of gravity. He found a new formula within the science of physics that explains the cause for, and the law which governs all falling objects. Today, everyone just 'knows' there is gravity! We share the 'knowledge,' the fruit of the investigation without having investigated it ourselves. Indeed, we likely forget how the concept of gravity came about; hence it is said that knowledge is borrowed or handed down.

Scientific theory progresses by designing models of reality and adjusting them when an accepted model fails to explain newly discovered aspects of the observed. An atom used to be pictured as having a solid core and one or more tiny particles called electrons circling it. Subsequently, this image of the atom, where electrons circle the core like planets the sun, was replaced by the electron cloud, and today an electron is considered to be a vibration instead of something solid, it is now seen as blinking in and out of existence. Once the original model was not able to explain new discoveries, it was modified. Even if one is not a specialized physicist who studies atoms, as a result of this continual pursuit, everyone has at least come across the notion of an atom as a very small particle.

Science pays attention to what can be observed and coins new words for what is discovered. This happens within a community of scientists and an environment of scientific discourse, which ideally, consists of open discussion and holds itself to standards of verifiability. This scientific discourse is rooted in exact definitions of scientific terms as the results of new discoveries are framed into new concepts. Those concepts then form new models of reality. Thus, we have gotten used to increasingly interpreting the world through those concepts as they enter the larger cultural consciousness. For example, we know a computer has a hard drive, but unless specializing in the field, most people don't have a clue how it works; every weather forecast utilizes radar, but how many people actually know what radar is? Thus, what we understand as 'the world' is a web of knowledge, or conceptual constructs, that are continuously handed down, modified, added to, refined, and become part of how everyone defines the world.

Models of Psychological Theory

Natural science explains the layers and workings of the natural environment through its concepts. Similarly, psychology seeks to explain—albeit without mathematical precision—how phenomena of the psyche are related and how the inner world works, by observing, formulating a theory, and presenting the result in the form of new concepts. Concepts in the humanities are less stringently defined than in natural science, hence there is a whole (and very old) discipline of interpreting and explaining them called hermeneutics. The latter interprets what is meant by a word by trying to establish the context in which it was used. This is also an issue in regard to spiritual terminology where we have simple words whose definitions cannot often be readily grasped because they are used in noncongruent way.

Psychology is widely looked upon as an approach that explains our inner universe, in other words, as explaining 'who we are' inside. For example, Jung came up with the notions of the collective unconscious and archetypes by studying dreams and myths. Before that, Freud analyzed the material his patients talked about and conceptualized the psychic structure of id/ego/super ego. He defined neurosis as what happens when one part is in conflict with another. The studies of his pupil Adler centered around his theory of the inferiority complex. He worked within the environment of the historical epoch of national socialism and his observations in that context shaped his concepts, for example, his ideas on the genesis of authoritarian character traits.

Psychological theory is a construct that is designed to provide a model of reality by sorting and classifying empirical psychological 'facts' and establishing their causalities within the specific theoretical frame. Like other sciences, especially in the humanities (e.g., economics, social or political theory), the different models build on preceding ones and are historically influenced. The current definition of depression, for example, has been shaped by the availability of mood enhancing drugs and their role within the pharmacological field. The prevailing milieu is very quick to label an uncomfortable inner state as depression and despite what it may be caused by, to then medicate it.

Concepts from such models also enter our pool of 'knowledge.' Today we speak of neurosis or inferiority complexes even though it is largely forgotten who coined the terms and in which context. Regardless, the concepts are then used to describe a set of behaviors or feelings. Sometimes it is comforting to have a conceptual frame for an experience. If some discomforting inner state has a name, such as traumatic stress syndrome, one may feel that one is not alone with it. Additionally, it can also be necessary to have a word symbol simply for the sake of communication.

If one seeks to explain one's psyche, or inner world, one has to keep in mind that all psychological theories are models, they interpret phenomena within their particular theory using language that has evolved within a particular theoretical frame. Psychology is a language-based activity that gives new meaning to or invents new words, in other words, it is an activity of conceptualization. This conceptualization establishes a kind of parallel reality—the concept points in a more or less coherent manner at something but is not the thing.

Concepts act as filters through which others and the self are viewed. Knowing a particular concept and then utilizing it is like applying borrowed, or handed down, knowledge. Even though it may appear advanced or knowledgeable, interpreting oneself through its prism and its framework is not the same as direct experience. Applying the concept is an afterthought, a categorization and interpretation of observed phenomena.

In the context of the theme of 'I'-Identification, such concepts can and often do become labels or classifications of the 'I' to which it attaches itself. In the past, according to distinctions within psychology, one may have been classified an oral or authoritarian character type, and using even older distinctions, a phlegmatic or a sanguine—all of these are concepts.

Psychological Labels

People who are on some kind of spiritual path have often also been engaged in other forms of inner exploration such as therapy, and if not, have probably read books about psychological topics. This is part of the avenue through which psychological terms find currency within spiritual communities and society at large. I want to cite a few relatively recent psychological concepts to show how such concepts have entered the public domain of normative language. One term is 'co-dependency.' It was originally coined to mean the specific challenges an alcoholic individual represents for his or her partner or spouse. It identifies such a relationship dynamic more precisely than the term 'relationship problems,' but lately, it has been used to describe relationship dynamics in general. In such a relationship dynamic, one person plays, for example, the role of victim. I think these days, most people know what is meant by the term victim in that context; it has become a psychological label.

Another term from psychological literature is 'toxic parents.' This term was introduced in the eighties and indicates that lack of self-esteem as well as other perceived dysfunctions in adulthood may have been caused by a parent's manipulative behavior. A theory which is currently quite popular, as well among spiritual friends in Germany, is 'family constellation' according to Bert Hellinger. It stresses the opposite of the 'toxic parent' model by stating that a person needs to respect every individual in the whole family system, going back several generations, in order to find peace. Both of these examples illustrate how theories can greatly differ by assigning a different cause to the same syndrome. Within Hellinger's model, the notion of 'fate' plays a large role, in the sense that it sees everyone standing in a long line of genetically predestined fate. It is quite interesting how people accept this when participating in such a group, and at the same time, if they are influenced by Advaita for example, also believe the exact opposite—that there is the possibility of liberation and that it comes from the recognition of not being the body. Because, if one is not the body, how can family be a fate and define who one is?

Another concept which emerged in the eighties is that of the 'inner child.' According to 'inner child' psychological theory, we suffer, to different degrees, from having an unloved, neglected 'child aspect,' and never quite recover from being emotionally malnourished. If someone has an understanding of what the 'inner child' concept entails, it is possible to communicate by saying, 'something is affecting my inner child.' The statement provides implied information about a hurtful feeling which is being experienced.

Psychological notions such as those highlighted can be used not only to describe and investigate what is actually happening, but can lead to using them as labels of the 'I,' thereby implying 'I am such.' For example, after attending family constellation and accepting its world view as a lens, one may say 'this or that is my fate' or 'I am this way because of my grandfather'; and after learning about co-dependency, one may say 'I am the victim.' The quoted examples are randomly chosen, and all the time, new examples appear in public consciousness, in the form of new psychological concepts. What is left out of the equation when using such labels—in this case psychological—is that they make a conceptual object out of inner phenomena and feeling states. One makes an object out of oneself, and simultaneously, one is made into an object by another person who is fluent in the terminology of the particular theory and who then categorizes the other through the prism of the theory.

We collectively make objects out of each other. We say things like 'you are not on time because your inner child is rebelling,' or 'you are mad because of such and such' (offering some smart theoretical concept). A lot of us have done some inward looking and turned to such theoretical explanations for what we found. For those who have engaged in meditation and psychotherapy, there is a propensity to look at oneself as an exemplification of the label that is currently in favor, for example, one gets 'objectified' as an enneagram six, or enneagram eight.

Conceptualizing the 'I' and its Classifications

When we take a psychological statement such as 'I have a trauma,' almost no one asks if there is something such as a trauma[25] or if there is an 'I' that can have it. It is simply presumed that both the 'I' and its classifications exist. Any conceptualization such as 'trauma' is an assumed understanding within a theoretical frame, and as such, is basically taken as valid in an a priori manner. There is then only a question of whether the 'I' has the trauma or not, or if it has this or that version. But the 'I' notion is itself already a concept.

I have wondered how many hours I've spent with friends discussing some new psychological theory, and then turned around and labeled one another according to its notions. I have attended many a meditation session where the final gong had barely quieted before we had gathered with our tea, busying ourselves by giving each other definitions such as teacher, disciple, meditator, and also esoteric ones like indigo person[26] or enneagram X. We believed we could be defined and often, that we should be defined—a good meditator is better than no meditator, a disciple better than no disciple. I am not sure how much of this mutual defining was interrupted by an awareness of how the 'I' is sustained by definitions. It has been said that 'thought' sustains the 'I.' This simply means that in the collective dreaming that goes on around and within everyone, there is the prevailing assumption that the 'I' is something that consists of attributes, and not surprisingly, psychological concepts are amongst some of its favored attributes.

The Empty Mirror and Prism Lenses

Labeling, using psychological and other personality concepts, cements the subject-object construct of an 'I' that has attributes, and consequently a world. As seen by the examples of newer psychological concepts that were cited, they all strive to explain a time-based cause and effect relationship between the past and how the 'I' turned out. This means they not only objectify 'us,' they also function, not so much as a mirror, but rather as a lens or prism. As soon as there is a bit of this kind of knowledge, there is a tendency to filter oneself and others through it. This is the basis of the view that the world is conceptual.

Since most psychological concepts state a cause and effect relationship between a past event and a current syndrome, they reinforce the sense that what one is, is a construct that has its roots in some past event. Additionally, any definition of the 'I' precludes its opposite; if I define myself as the inner child, I am, to that extent, less defined by being an adult, perhaps only later when the 'hurt child' condition is remedied. If I am in bondage, I am not free. If I am full of unconscious patterns, I cannot be properly conscious at the same time. Hence, the pattern is to first define myself as psychologically wanting, and then task myself with changing that condition. This is instead of refraining from the attachment to the definition in the first place. If I believe what I am is an enneagram type, then I suffer because I am stuck on being enneagram X and see no means of escape from the definition. This is a condition I found myself in at one time—first believing that what I am is enneagram X and then suffering from 'being' it. This is one example of how the 'I' elaborately re-creates itself as its own trap.

Still, what goes on in the phenomenal time-space reality can be observed and described, so sometimes it is useful to play with the description without making a prescription out of it. For example, Myers-Briggs[27] suggests that the natural manner of inner processing for an extrovert is through constant talking, for an introvert through being alone. This type of information can be helpful for parents or for anyone who has been puzzled about how someone else functions. On a personal level, if for example someone tries to make progress with meditation only and feels as if they've been treading water for years, they may try a more flexible attitude and derive some benefit from working with a personality model such as the enneagram.

The enneagram is a personality typology consisting of nine types. It is not based on static traits but on the observation of the particular dynamic through which each type functions. At the root of this dynamic is the existential wound of being separate from the divine source—the same underlying condition within everyone. This condition is one of pain and lack.

The different types come about as each individual develops a specific way of reacting to this condition and it has been found that there are nine particular ways of reaction: withdrawing, helping, chasing perfection, accumulating things, being skeptical, mistaking emotional drama for aliveness, taking refuge in power, avoiding conflict, and being addicted to image. The enneagram can give good insights regarding one's inner dynamics when specific circumstances trigger specific questions. It is a good tool for explaining why there is such deep despair sometimes and how a lot of people face this layer. Presentations of the enneagram vary greatly. I happen to like the one by H. A. Almaas because he sees it within the context of spiritual work.[28]

Everything can be useful on the way; and then nothing is useful. Ultimately, everyone will come to the point when inner work fails. Until then, it is helpful if there is an understanding of what models do or don't do. They can help one distinguish the phenomenal when a solid feedback loop to the observed is established, but, they can also impose their conceptual form on the phenomenal. The manifold nature of appearance includes all theories—reality is all-inclusive. The journey is full of contradictions and paradoxes.

The Model of Astrology

In addition to looking at psychology to explain 'what is happening with us,' astrology can add a different angle. I mention it here because it is an area of interest for people who are inclined towards self-exploration. It is a reality model that can be turned into another layer of self-classification, as in, 'as Libra I am such.' Astrology seeks to explain the dynamics of life by assigning meanings to the planets, viewing them as metaphors for certain tendencies. How useful this approach is at a certain time and for a specific situation depends on the individual astrologer, on how well she or he has grasped the theory and its applications, and how well he or she can communicate information to a client.

Sometimes one struggles with an issue for which one cannot find a resolution, but which, through a well-founded astrological analysis can be seen in a different light. Astrology addresses patterns and themes which, when interpreted correctly, are indicative of more fundamental levels of acting forces of reality than some emotional theories. Exploring astrological ideas and interpretations may provide the opportunity to 'interpret' phenomena in a way that is different from what one had assumed. For example, psychology may not have an explanation why a particular life issue feels so leaden and stagnant, or why one's world seems turned upside down by a chain of sudden events, while a good astrologer may provide helpful hints.[29]

In astrology, the main concepts such as planets and related aspects are metaphors. Astrology is a symbolic language in which the meaning of the symbols is very wide and leaves room for a lot of flux. Earlier it was mentioned how a particular thought can bring about an emotion, that is, the mental layer of functioning can influence the emotional layer. This process goes the other way as well, an emotion can stimulate the intuitive layer of thinking using pictures and analogies; these work by approximation rather than through strict definition. They are less logical and more metaphorical, so they will not appeal to a very rational mind.

The model of astrology can describe, in its own 'symbolic' way, tendencies within phenomenal reality. For example, Richard Tarnac has examined historical epochs going back many hundreds of years and looked at their particular scientific discoveries, social movements, and art.[30] He correlated them with patterns of the prevalent planetary cycles. He points out how the Uranus-Pluto aspect of the sixties tells us something about that era, as it indeed coincides with revolutionary upheaval, emancipatory impulses, and radical cultural innovation. In the beginning of the twenty-first century, a very different quality pervades, and we have all experienced it. Tarnac describes this period as one of contraction, empowerment of reactionary forces and totalitarian impulses, one of gravity, tension, crisis, and the feeling of an 'end of an era.' The particular aspect of the Pluto & Saturn cycle at this time provides the language that characterizes its main tendencies. As with large-scale themes, when used with care and deep insight, the language of astrology can also describe tendencies on a personal level. Still, these descriptions are classifications of the phenomenal and therefore cannot tell anyone who they are.

Chakra Theory as Esoteric Knowledge

Another model which seeks to describe our inner functioning is that of chakras, that is, energy centers. There isn't just one theory of chakras; depending on the model consulted, we have seven, or eight, or twelve, or even hundreds of chakras.[31] Chakra theory originated in India and describes 'energy' flow within the body-mind including very subtle levels of functioning for which Western science has no frame of reference. The theory objectifies phenomena which can be perceived internally by naming them in specific ways and sorting them according to the model. It can be helpful, for example when someone comes to know that a hot burning sensation in the third eye is not a rare occurrence when meditating, he or she can be reassured.

Learning about chakras, in the sense of studying the Sanskrit terminology and the functions of chakras through books, is an academic pursuit. But being fluent in the language of chakra theory does not mean one is spiritually more advanced. As mentioned above, constantly interpreting and objectifying oneself through the lens of this or other theories is not helpful. One may believe in a concept of kundalini and then wait for certain inner happenings that are then interpreted as kundalini phenomena. Awareness includes awareness of the tendency to hanker for such phenomena, as well as the use of the model's language to communicate about them when appropriate.

When it comes to subtle inner phenomena, it is useful to have a frame of reference for explaining what may be happening. Western knowledge is very spotty in this regard. In the West, we have remained with our psychological references when it comes to understanding 'who we are inside.' In the East, over thousands of years, people have meditated and have observed the inner world. The kind of knowledge that has resulted from such inner observation has been dubbed 'esoteric.' But it is still knowledge about something; it is interpretative language concerning how phenomena relate to each other.

Chakra pictures are often very aesthetic, with all their triangles and lotuses and rays of color, and they can inspire creative visualization. But chakra theory reinforces the idea of growth in stages, and the knowledge it imparts is conceptual.

Spiritual Models as Concepts Regarding Truth

To the extent that spiritual teachings employ language, they also behave as conceptual prisms and are therefore unable to convey the inconceivable. On the level of language and thinking, information that says there is a realm beyond thinking can be communicated. Such information may even point to a dimension called 'absolute.' But for knowing oneself, or cognizing this 'absolute' about which nothing can be known, there needs to be the immediacy of experience without labeling, a letting go of the coveted object, even if the object is called 'the teaching.'

Spiritual models are interwoven concepts within a certain environment. Within certain spiritual discourses, it is sometimes said that someone experiences 'inner spaciousness.' But even this is a concept, and concepts exist in clusters that mutually create their meaning. In other environments, no one would value or understand the concept of spaciousness, but in spiritual circles, it is regarded as a positive occurrence, something that can even be wished for.

Non-duality is another concept or model of reality that is increasingly popular. While pointing to a truth, its discussion can become very academic and philosophical, and somebody who can speak knowledgeably about it may not have experienced it existentially. Here also, it can be forgotten that the concept is not the thing. Even the tenets of non-duality can be used to make oneself or the other into exemplifications that see the concept as an object. That is, it is possible to say 'I am one' while viewing this oneness as a classification of the 'I' or even a wishful assumption. In this way, it is even possible to discuss whether someone exemplifies true oneness or a oneness which is still lacking, and to forget that oneness implies that it is neither this nor that, that it is neither a quality or an attribute of a 'someone.'

Models Are Not Reality

According to the Chinese Five Elements theory, there are five emotions that in turn correspond to five organs, elements, and colors. Another system that works with emotions and is known as the Sedona method, postulates nine emotions. I have also worked with a list of over twenty emotions. Obviously models can be looked at as being grounded in empirical observation. This also explains why some models find certain phenomena more important than others. At the same time, the examples illustrate how if someone takes a model as reality, the learned knowledge can become the perceived reality, in this case, one could posit that I (or you) have five emotions, or nine, or x emotions—the model says so, so it must be the case. Again, this is objectifying oneself as an exemplification of the model, resulting in a belief about how one is.

As homo sapiens, we use symbols, we experience ourselves on the level of conceptual knowledge, and we enjoy engaging with knowledge. But no knowledge can reach to the dimension of who one is, hence if one likes to engage with a certain theory, who is there to object and look down on such a pastime, if it resonates with a person? We can examine which theories are not holding up to empirical verification, and which ones do not bother with it at all. It would be a bankruptcy of our discerning and thinking ability to throw every theory into the same basket by saying all are concepts and to neglect that there are qualitative differences amongst them. Some of the more esoteric ones are nothing but fantasy while others are woefully incomplete or simply incompetent.

All this is part of the show. Consciousness plays the role of the theory, the practitioner, the client; it plays the role of the theoreticist who presents his discovery and the *advocatus diaboli* who questions it, as well as the listener who enjoys this dialogue. It also plays the role of those little bottles of perfume which supposedly contain the essence of ascended masters, of the one who likes their smell, as well as the one who laughs at the idea of the master in the bottle, and who knows, maybe it plays the master in the bottle.

Awareness reflects what is going on in interpretative thinking as well as beyond it, in the other layers of the body-mind, the realm of the heart for example. As far as I can tell, it does not take sides for or against thinking or even conceptualization as such. It has been called the empty mirror because it does not label. It has no preferences and has no more or less informed theoretical concepts, and no preferred path.

9

Spirituality for Hire

The utilitarian trait of the mind is predominant today, possibly more openly than in other times. The Western culture of individualism focuses on the idea that life is there for the purpose of a 'me' and its satisfaction. When it finds itself in conditions that it deems unsatisfactory, the 'I' wants to change the world and itself according to its wishes, easily succumbing to the idea that this is a worthwhile pursuit. Apart from the fact that this is a wheel that keeps turning, and more is never enough, the ideologies which nowadays promote 'doability' invariably have a component that is deemed 'spiritual.'

The Path of Discernment

A long time ago I heard a spiritual master using a metaphor that although a beautiful palace can be reached, one builds huts along the way and wants to settle there. When I heard this I swore to myself that I would never stop and build a hut, but go on and find out what is at the end of the road. Yet, unable to wake from the dream of 'myself,' attempting to build one of those huts was just what I set out to do.

Anything to do with healing, spirituality, and the functioning of the body-mind had always been close to my heart. Over a period of many years there had been a number of educational trainings, learning first about the physical body and then the energetic or emotional body. After working for years in a field that did not coincide with those interests, I intended a professional switch into the area of body mind healing. I was ever looking for a better understanding and a method that I would find suitable to use with others. With a measure of envy, I sometimes met people who had learned one modality and became a practitioners of it, while instead, I was moved to investigate ever deeper aspects of the body-mind. When my attention finally turned to the mental layer of limiting beliefs and personality structure, I believed this to be the approach that would address everyone's issues the best.

Increasingly, I believed in the concept of personal development, the notion that if only enough self-limiting patterns were dissolved, a person's life would blossom into richness. Only in hindsight did it become obvious to what extent this belief in the notion of personal expansion had been influenced by a whole contemporary movement outside of me. The ideology of self-development was, and still is, in vogue.

From the context of meditation to which I had been exposed, I remember the saying that the best way of finding freedom is to get to the root of the mind, but it was still a mystery what was exactly meant by that. And if I could not be in no-mind, then at least it seemed better to strive for a mind that ran efficiently without any 'energy leaks' or 'self defeating patterns.' Within contemporary ideology there was no shortage of approaches that promised just that. My heartfelt intention was to investigate what worked and what did not. I may have heard talk of 'oneness' during that time, but it was of little interest to me. What was sought was a redemption that made life better by making the mind better, but I never quite succeeded in getting beyond all its unconscious and less-desired mechanisms.

Just recently I read Susan Segal's autobiography *Collision with the Infinite*,[32] in which she describes how even in the mid-nineties in California, academic psychology pathologized everything. Her therapists and colleagues diagnosed the fact that she did not live from the 'I' perspective as a neurotic problem that needed the remedy of psychotherapy. Around that time, a profession called 'Coaching' emerged in the US, and it may well be that its wider appeal was a reaction to the tendency of psychology to pathologize. As far as I was concerned, I was fed up with looking at what was wrong, and finally wanted to look at what was right and healthy and possible. Subsequently, after I signed up for such a coaching training course, one of the first things we were told was that psychology deals with the (hurtful) past and coaching with the (hopeful) future.

I did not question the underlying belief in an 'I' that should and could be transformed—if only done right, with an appropriate method, and a great degree of insight into what was going on with a client. I became greatly invested in the idea of self-development, fascinated by its emerging techniques, and soon found myself caught in its ideological maze. What I call an ideology is a cluster or web of ideas that cloud perception and steer thinking and action. While models of reality—psychological, astrological, and even the chakra model—strive for a measure of empirical verification and a feedback loop between their hypotheses and observed phenomena, an ideology moves farther away from empirical data, not bothering much with empirical confirmation. It takes on the cloak of a belief system and sets up its own reality.

The exposure to key notions of the self-development move-ment put me on a path that resembled a tightrope walk between puzzlement and confusion on one side, and trying to discern what was true on the other. This was especially so because without exception, all techniques, approaches, and methods that I encountered made claims towards being spiri-tual. In fact, nowadays there seems to be even more of a cross-over between those who engage in self-improvement exercises while also following a kind of spiritual path influ-enced by notions of 'awakening.'

What Is Spirituality?

The more I heard spirituality mentioned—and it is mentioned everywhere these days—the more confused I got about what it meant. There was often puzzlement when people declared that either they or someone else is spiritual as a kind of factual statement. When I heard that, I wondered how they could be so sure. At the same time, it was increasingly evident that everyone understands something different by it. Some believe in or have had experiences of a higher power, divine guidance, or angels, and thereby consider themselves spiritual. By the same token, others believe in aliens, reincarnation, spirit beings or disembodied guides, or they practice meditation, and also consider themselves spiritual. Then there are those for whom their experience of spirituality unfolds in the context of traditional religious beliefs. In this global age especially, at least in Western countries, we are free to concoct our very own spiritual mix from a huge bazaar of goods; we can be with Peruvian shamans one week, in a Thai monastery the next, then round off the trip with a visit to a holy site in India.

Even dictionaries are not much help in defining spirituality because they mostly explain 'spirituality' by 'spiritual' and vice versa—explaining the same with the same. But no matter what definition is offered, spirituality is usually considered an attribute of a person, a label such as holy, generous, refined, a supremely desirable attribute, more special than anything of a materialistic nature. And even though the preferred spiritual orientation is quite personal, people can get really attached to their ideas of what spiritual is and get defensive if their idea is challenged. To add to the confusion, the same word also refers to the understanding of self-realization in the Eastern sense.

Dr. Wayne Dyer, a contemporary inspirational writer and lecturer, says for example, "Your inner knowing is that you are not the body, its mind, or any of its achievements or possessions."[33] This sounds good so far, but then he goes on: "You are an infinite spiritual being," "this shift of seeing yourself as a spiritual being ..."[34] This way of speaking implies that there is an 'I' that gets even better by being infinite and spiritual. It is typical of how contemporary ideology incorporates the idea of spirituality as an attachment of the person while really subsuming it under the ego agenda. It is hard not to be lulled into a trance by these kinds of texts because they suggest that it is the 'I' that holds the universal, eternal, infinite, that there is a 'me' that is the container of the divine. It is almost like opium, a propaganda that is accepted without investigation if one hears it often enough. I remember waiting for the divine to finally pour itself into 'me' and this may have been the case with others as well.

To say 'I am spiritual' equals the attempt of the mind to usurp territory about which it knows absolutely nothing, a grandiose gesture of posturing. This very basic distortion shows up in almost all of the self-development approaches. In the first place, it is the mind itself that distinguishes what is 'spiritual' from the 'non-spiritual.' The 'I' causes the apparent separation. Meanwhile, life is all-inclusive, and if anything, it is the mind and the 'I' that are contained in the great universal vastness and not the other way round. A plastic cup cannot contain the ocean. The very identification with the limited 'I' is what causes the perceived lack and consequent desire for something bigger, and the biggest prize of all is to be universal, eternal, divine. If the former is dropped, the gambit of the prize disappears with it, then there is only one whole.

Spirituality as 'Part' of Us

Not long after a broader interest in Eastern spirituality started permeating the Western cultural experience, spirituality also started showing up in psychological methods. The new aspect of spirit entered the scope of psychological methodology and the new approach that incorporated such a facet is known as Integrative psychology. At first sight, this sounds really good, holistic, and closer to the truth of what one is—honoring a person in all that she or he is. It means one is no longer just looking at oneself as a neurotic syndrome of unconscious drives that do battle with the conscious ones and cause misery, one now has at least a part that is light-filled and spiritual.

The component of spirit is added as a constituent of the structure of the psyche, with the other constituents being the physical, the emotional (unconscious), and the conscious. It is interesting to see how sometime during the course of history, Freud's model of the psyche has been modified, because only the id and ego are now left. A physical dimension has been added while the notion of the super ego has been let go of. This indicates a significant shift for the historical development of psychology in the hundred years since Freud. It points to a change in how the 'spiritual' dimension is collectively perceived, and also how the modern psyche sees itself as being less under the restrictive force of authority than in the past. Freud interpreted the God of religion as an infantile reaction to the father image and as a function of the super ego. In the model of integrative psychology, the super ego that produces the belief in this kind of God in the first place, has disappeared. Instead, we have a higher power or spirit in its place. That spirit is a part of what constitutes what we are instead of being something out there; it forms an integrative part of the human psyche and is seen as a benevolent guiding force that intimately belongs to us.

Psychological approaches within integrative psychology introduce this 'spiritual part' and strive to provide guidance in how to embrace it. The Quadrinity process is an example of a method that is based on the model that views human beings as consisting of four parts, hence 'quadrinity.' It was created in the seventies around the same time the notion of humanistic or integrative psychology first showed up. It is a therapeutic process compressed into eight days of group residence utilizing a very tightly structured and participatory process that requires substantial financial investment and a solid motivation and commitment. I participated in it only a few years ago, long after it was founded.[35]

In chapter five I mentioned how one is entranced by one's life story, and how the increased intensity of a group process can be very compelling because the story is intensified. Despite the fact that the acknowledgment of spirit initially sounded good, after I participated in Quadrinity, something did not feel quite right, and for a long time I was not able to put a finger on it. Feeling a need to discern, I had another look at the fundamental assumptions that are at play in it. Basically, it says that we have four aspects—physical, unconscious, conscious, and spirit—and that these aspects interact and can be aligned.[36] Apart from the fact that it is not clearly defined how those 'aspects' relate, the assumed basics are as follows: (a) we have a self, (b) the self has four parts, (c) one of those 'parts' is spirit, and (d), one is 'whole' if those 'parts' are integrated. It is implied that participation in the process makes this integration happen.

It can now be seen more clearly how the model's concepts filter one's world view, or in other words, what the model propagates about what we are. First, it postulates a self, and then that this self consists of four parts. In reality there is no self as an independent entity, so it cannot have any parts. To say there is a self with parts is the postulation of an idea. To say spirit is a part of the self depends on the postulation of a self, and logically, it also depends on the postulation that there is indeed something called spirit. If both do not exist, the whole concept collapses into nothing, a nothingness that is unlikely to keep the illusory bubble of any psychological method going.

Quadrinity and other processes like it imply that because spirituality is addressed—whatever is meant by it—a potential outcome of the process is 'spiritual awakening.' The term 'spiritual awakening' has been used to mean a lot of different things. I have read a definition that said that during the last fifty years there was a spiritual awakening because increasingly, people are more aware of subtle layers of perception, such as their intuitive sense, or their right brain functions. Another states that 'awakening' is the discovery of inner qualities such as wisdom—even perfect wisdom—guidance, or a loving spiritual aspect. It should be noted how 'spiritual awakening' is used in a lot of different meanings, but how in the context of inner development it does often does not mean the same as in the context of Advaita—it often has nothing to do with self-realization. To me, it seemed that 'spirituality' had been somehow adopted into the terminology of inner growth and given hopelessly twisted meanings until hardly anyone knew what was meant.

If someone has an understanding that spiritual awakening actually means ceasing to believe in the concept of an 'I,' or realizing that there is no 'I,' how could this happen within a conceptual frame that promotes such a belief in the first place? This is a good example of the pitfall of engaging in inner work that is guided by wrong notions. I referred to the Quadrinity example because I personally experienced it and because at first, it sounds so sensible and promising, that is, until it creates a conceptual maze that is difficult to cognize. Because everyone who engages in it—group members and leaders alike—fundamentally has to believe in it, the difficulty of penetrating through the veils that surround the collectively accepted reality can be a challenge.

While the self-discovery movement was in the beginning driven by sheer interest in experimentation itself, it gradually morphed into a means to an end, a means of facilitating some kind of gain. For example, in reference to Quadrinity, this is how the goal is described: "Those who come to the Hoffman Quadrinity Process have a strong commitment to making changes ... and to accelerating their personal growth and development."[37] The East gave us the idea that the ego must be the reason for our troubles, while contemporary Western ideology, in a very strange twist, is insistently telling us the ego (sometimes called self), can and should change and 'grow,' and that 'spirituality' provides it with even more 'accelerated' and better growth.

The Basic Tenet in 'Coaching'—the 'I'

Originally, I was drawn to familiarizing myself with coaching because I saw some benefit in looking at a life situation outside the usual framework of friends, colleagues, and family. I saw some benefit in mulling something over without filtering it through automatically operating preconceived notions, and to conducting such exploratory dialogue with an attitude of curiosity and openness. What the coaching program contained, though, were a number of ideological concepts I was unable to subscribe to. Still, as even these come from the eternal hide and seek play of consciousness, so is the impulse to question them.

As with other facets of the inner growth movement, 'spirituality' was established within the coaching program as a class bearing the same title. This sounded quite progressive, but like integral psychology, what was understood as spirituality was very general. Spirituality was whatever was believed, and whatever was believed belonged to the category. Spirituality was not seen as having anything to do with truth, and increasingly, I had an uncomfortable feeling that spirituality was being hijacked and made into an attachment of the ego by this and other methods of the self-development movement.

The basic purpose of coaching was taught to center around the questions "What do you want to have?" and "Who do you want to be?" If anyone resonates, in any way at all, with the understanding that asking the question 'who am I' is central to leading one out of illusion by stripping away all ideas of oneself and leaving one standing naked, it is easy to see that the starting point within coaching is incompatible with this understanding. The coaching activity is instead concerned with the qualities and possessions of the 'I.' It is about making the 'I' more important, more solid, more impressive, and pretending to give it success and fulfilment.

What is of interest here is the 'I' as possessor, the belief not only that 'you' can have success, but that it is the coach who gives it to you. At the same time, the motivation to enter coaching, from the viewpoint of a client, is a result of the reactivity of the mind to 'what is.' That mind wants to change things, and coaching is just another approach in a long line of attempts to have the world shaped according to one's desires. The longer I was exposed to those notions, the more it felt that they consisted of leading someone down the wrong path. One has to ask, therefore, if such coaching does not, at best, constitute a huge detour. By encouraging attachment to the temporal and propagating some future 'fulfilment,' it seems to contradict the perspective of a truth of being, the idea that the only fulfilment is in being itself. Seeking to improve one's life conditions may be an appropriate endeavor under certain circumstances, but I had a dim sense that the implicit world view of coaching institutionalized a running into dead ends at great speed and with blind excitement.

To the extent that a coaching program is conceived for the purpose of professional training, or as a supplemental education, it can and should be evaluated according to the appropriate criteria. The critique here is only concerned with some of the core ideological concepts in as much as they contradicted the understanding of the notion of spiritual awakening (in the Eastern sense of the word). It was only long after being involved in it that I could examine them with greater clarity. My remarks are based on the ideology, and are not a value judgment on whether situation-specific coaching can be useful.[38]

Susceptibility to Self-Improvement

Everyone experiences dissatisfactions in one way or another. They appear in countless ways for each individual and are triggered by a whole host of life situations. Deep down, at the root, lies the nagging discontent due to not knowing who one is, identification with constricted life conditions and other temporal manifestations, and the identification with the idea of being a separate autonomous 'I.' These dissatisfactions come from resistance to 'what is'. All too often, life conditions are less than ideal, and at other times, lacking, painful, or empty—hence the wide susceptibility of people to the message that 'things can be better.'

Investigation of the message that 'things can get better' and its implications can also be accomplished within a general cultural critique of zeitgeist, for example the more powerless individuals become, the more they may cling to the hope for personal power. It is addressed here insofar as it pairs up with how the idea of spirituality fits into that dream. While psychological methods respond primarily to the need of relieving inner pressure and pain and have present experience as a departure point, self-development methods hook into the wish and desire for a change for the 'better.' These days, it is rare for someone to not be buying into the vision of a 'better life.' In order to make it happen—whatever it is—spirituality is conceived of as the magic ingredient and the means to the end. Very often, the idea of the 'better life' is packaged in a way that includes the desire for inner qualities such as joy and love, as if they can be had for a price.

'You Can Have What You Want'

The notion of 'who you want to be' that is formulated within coaching, and within other manifestations of the self-improvement world, bypasses taking a look at what is, at who one is, and institutes a movement away from what is, which is either conceived of as not ok or not enough, and presupposes a personal doer who will remedy the predicament. By concerning itself with 'what one wants,' a method is only attractive in as far as it displays credibility at making such wants possible. There is an underlying assumption that (a) one can indeed have what one wants, and (b) that the particular method (coaching, motivational teacher, 'how to' book, etc.) can actually deliver the results.

Most practitioners within the field of self-development use some variation of the 'you can have what you want' theme to sell their work. They advertise themselves as having the ability to give it to you and this strikes a chord within people because most are sitting on a shifting pile of wants. It has been quipped in psychological circles that the world is run by four year olds because at that age the ego structure has been formed. This makes one wonder whether the insistence on the theme of 'having what you want' within the motivational industry is not indicative of two-year-olds who have not learned the lesson that the world does not revolve around their wishes.

The claim that 'you can have what you want' is so general that few people pause to consider whether it is true; of course, the more general a claim, the less specific the content, and empirical proof is often neglected. A whole industry is being powered by this claim, and by employing emphatic repetition, the credo is dressed up as a fact. Instead of questioning the assumption, a person may be led to feel he or she just lacks self-determination or suffers from too much self-doubt. And the implied solution?—invest in more programs and seminars or strategies to eliminate the perceived flaw.

All of this activity is fueled by a desire to create the world according to one's wishes even when these are glorified as 'visions' of the future. The activity is fueled by hope, and hope is a projection into the future, even though in reality, the things or situations that are wanted and hoped for are a continuation of the past since any idea of what is wanted is informed by what happened before.

There is also a belief that one's 'wants' manifest even better when one is a spiritual person. But if there is really an understanding how the temporal world is fleeting, and how one's being is beyond it, then why invest so much in the dream? If one realizes oneself prior to all time, this gives an immediacy to everything—there is just being with what is and no energy for hoping or wanting, no need for any strategies because what is, is suchness. When the 'I' is revealed as the insubstantial fiction it really is, one hard-to-describe surprise is that the ego has gained absolutely nothing. It used to believe that it needed to be transformed, more fulfilled, beautified, purified, or otherwise prepared for an 'awakening' that it believed to be a material addition to itself, but this is not so. Awakening changes nothing materially, there is not even anyone there to be more loving because love is all that is.

The Wish-Fulfilling Treadmill

As with the example of the Quadrinity process, methods of 'inner growth' have concerned themselves ever less with finding out just what is happening, and increasingly, with pursuing a means to an end. Some of the goal descriptions now include 'moving a client forward', whereby one has to wonder whether either practicioner or client know where this 'forward' is. Another example of this are the number of psychologists in the US as well as Europe who now use the word 'coaching' to describe their work, with the focus of this work being understood to be a method of 'helping achieve this and that goal.' Often, the goals are determined from the kind of 'vision' one is encouraged to come up with, that is, conceptualize for one's life.

Wants, goals and visions—all are, to an extent, influenced by what is already known. They are reactions to a remembered past projected into the future—one wishes for either more or less of what has already happened. The purpose of this activity is not how to step out of the wheel of desires, but to keep striving and becoming and changing and having success, so that sometime, maybe, in the distant future, one can sit back. Meanwhile, the ideology of obtaining a better life keeps pushing one to act on 'getting there,' bypassing livingness and the living intelligence which is already happening. Life—something easy to forget—is a verb and not a noun; as a noun, it is a stagnant, static concept.

Livingness is alive and does not succumb to what is wanted by an individual; it follows its own living game plan. It is in constant flux, like Heraclitus said,[39] and includes a never-ending cycle of change from one form to the next—creating, sustaining, and destroying—the cycle of all phenomenal things.[40] Participating fully in this livingness would mean opening oneself up to it, being carried by it and trusting its wisdom, instead of missing most of it by trying to mold it into one's ideas of what it should be.

Being Stuck on Self-Definition

In a book titled *Flow*[41], after interviewing scores of people from all walks of life, the author observes that happiness happens when a person is absorbed in what they are doing, when they are actually forgetting themselves. In contrast, methods of self-development install a constant mechanism of self-definition. One is permanently and mentally preoccupied with wondering 'what are my wants; do I move forward; how do I move forward; is there success; how can I have more?' or even the mental gymnastics of 'was I happy, did I forget myself?'

This amounts to an implicit project of looking at oneself as an object, constantly checking how one measures up through the particular prism of 'how I want to see myself and be seen.' One is almost compulsively dwelling on whether desired outcomes are manifesting.

How did it come about that the unpopularity of 'being in one's mind' was replaced, so soon, by such a pervasive mental defining and redefining of oneself? In the coaching training which I underwent, a great amount of time was spent with such redefining, and this was mostly a purely verbal reframing and renaming, for example, calling something a 'shift' instead of a 'change.'

There is a great concern with the 'I' and its qualifications when it comes to self-definition that despite all the touting of some spiritual aspect, the ideology becomes an utter distortion of how the functioning of the ego-mind and the truth which we are relate; it morphs into a program of self-interest. Illustrating this self-interest are popular catchphrases such as 'you deserve better,' 'master your destiny' or 'increase your personal power.' In reality, one does not have to look far to see that one does not really have much power over circumstances, or over one's own actions, or even over the details of one's inner journey or over what happens within the next hour. The sooner the basic powerlessness is accepted, the better. I have to say, though, that I did not learn this lesson easily. In hindsight, I have asked myself if I could have avoided some of the struggles by being more accepting. Still, it is a moot issue because everything happens the way it is supposed to, and accepting this, also includes accepting the complete inability to accept, of occasionally wanting to get out of or away from what is.

Breathless Striving versus Being Here Now

Sometimes, the ideological notions highlighted are delivered together with a counter-contemplative breathlessness—a characteristic of the trance-inducing techniques which are employed in the field. Those do not allow space for reflecting about the relative truth of what is being presented, nor space for questioning or for informed dialogue about the validity of the premises and methods. The latter would be basic to any valid scientific approach. Additionally, some catchy notions of self-development are presented as leading to the fulfillment of some 'potential,' and as noted, with the latter being conceived as a quality of an 'I' and as some future 'thing.' The proposed path 'onward towards the potential' is pretty much the opposite of any kind of meditative approach.

The moment which is alive *now* is not part of the potential dream, it actually cannot be; the latter has no room in it, being nothing but a hopeful phantom. This can be seen just by watching. But if one is captured by the idea of getting to the potential goal, one is already in the impulse of wanting to get away from the present. The best that can be done is to recognize this reactivity and embrace it as the present condition. To try 'not to be reactive' is a recipe that only prolongs the reaction by being a reaction to the reaction.

10

Nothing Works

No recipe works. If there was one, its secret ingredients would be known by now. Even the attempt at refraining from recipes is equally a recipe and does not work either. Only 'no thing' works, that which is never a thing, what one is already and what in language appears nevertheless, as a thing.

Strategies Disappear

During the time when I attended the coaching program and was exposed to the lingo of this and similar ideologies, my main focus was on becoming certified in a therapeutic approach that had originally seemed very intriguing. Similar to the premises of the Quadrinity process, it postulated four aspects—conscious, bodily, unconscious, and soul—and integrated many healing techniques and insights derived from personality models. It was a very 'client-centered' approach, stressing that the individual be seen as one whole. However, I remember sitting in the study room when almost imperceptibly the question arose whether this whole intricate body-mind model or method was 'part of the solution or part of the delusion.'

There was a doubt forming, not because this particular method was inferior, but because I started wondering whether it was necessary to first see oneself as having all those complicated unconscious patterns in order to then proceed and solve them. I wondered whether diagnosing unconscious patterns 'as defined by the method' pointed to something real or whether it was already a fiction, a fiction which the model and thereby the therapist, propagated first in order to remedy it subsequently.

I increasingly wondered if everything that was done within the session was meant to solve something that was not there in the first place, or to put it differently, whether it was necessary to believe in the method's world view first, in order to practice it. I was less and less able to live by the understanding that as therapist or facilitator, one has a true grasp of what is going on, despite the advanced information with specialized knowledge. More and more it felt that such a conceptual approach would even take away some of the dignity of a person or client, and at best, the procedures which were prescribed started to resemble some kind of entertainment. The method in question was a very structured model and its therapeutic process followed a very strict protocol, and as such, it ran counter to what was mentioned earlier about the benefits of non-dual psychotherapy which starts and operates on the premise of non-knowing.

In hindsight, at that time I was moving beyond all methods even as I was proceeding to finish the training. I have since become aware that this is a typical moment on the path, when anything that has worked before does not work anymore. If someone has worked a lot with methods, whether primarily psychological or meditative, this can be very unsettling. In order to convince myself to complete the program, the voice of doubt was being put on the back burner, but how could I base work with a client on something I did not see as true anymore?

As mentioned earlier, in spiritual circles it is sometimes heard that it is better to go to the root of the mind than to engage with the mind. By that time and by being in this field, it became more obvious how the mind creates methods to fix itself. Doubt in any mind-based therapy arose from immersing myself precisely in such methods. It seems a very long detour to take but who can argue with life itself?

From the current vantage point, it looks very absurd that a construct such as the 'mind' would be able to solve a problem that it itself creates. The mind is a concept consisting of memory, interpretation, and belief in a past-to-future continuum. Possibly because it senses what a paper dragon it is, it tries to subsume everything under its pompous rulership, even the solutions to problems that exist only in its fantasy, such as my former beliefs about 'unconscious patterns' and other theoretical constructs.

I had reached a point where I could not induce a client into believing he or she actually had the patterns that this particular method detected. This made it impossible to practice the method, and to play the role of 'practitioner'. Slowly, without being able to put it into these words at the time, I had drifted away from believing that the 'I' is something that should or even could be qualified, not even with intricately conceived inner patterns of the unconscious kind.[42]

When there is self-knowledge, in the sense of knowing oneself as being the one source, it is clear that the mind, by perpetuating the time-based 'I'-idea, obscures the reality of who one is. It is therefore quite absurd that the mind could be a guide out of time-based problems at the same time. This would be like believing the thick fog when it says it is the one that will show the stars, or believing the dark lampshade when it claims that it is the one that will flood everything with light. Mind-based strategies will never get to the root of the mind, hence, methods, techniques, or strategies that are designed by the mind and therefore ensure its continuation are not an option. They are tantamount to 'looking for the needle outside the house after it has been lost inside.'[43]

Disintegration of 'My' World

As my doubts surmounted, life took turns that were strange and upsetting, as well as devastating and disheartening. Instead of nicely building on a solid professional base and seeing the fruition of all this inner work in spiritual and other fulfilment, 'my' world seemed to be disintegrating slowly and painfully. This lasted for years.

Relationships with others dissolved in strange and inexplicable ways, one after the other, until it felt as if I did not exist. I literally felt out of place in whatever physical location I found myself in. There were challenges that seemed less like opportunities for growth and more like bricks thrown at my feet. They were all the more unsettling as I was unable to put them in a context of 'this is what I have to learn; although it is challenging, I will be better off for it.' Circumstances seemed perpetually adverse. There was the distinct sense that 'my world' was crumbling away from me. Nothing made sense, I just could not 'do' the way I used to. One friend said 'Oh, you are capable, why don't you just do this or that,... why don't you just ...' I only knew that I couldn't. I did not have words for it then, but in hindsight the sense of control was dissipating. I was desperate for some meaning in all this, hoping that bouts

of terror and pain would diminish if only I could understand
them.

After some time during which everything seemed to glide
away, I spoke to an intuitively gifted astrologer friend. Her first
sentence mirrored my inner state precisely when she said
"You are standing in the fog; you can see no more than a foot
in front of you, if that. Life is grinding you down and there is
nothing you can do." She also said this would last for several
years, that astrologically there was no indication anything
would change soon at all. I cried, and then cried some more as
I found myself without the comforting idea of there being land
in sight in the near future. It felt as if I would cease to exist by
the mechanism of some strange decompression, and 'years'
seemed like an eternity which only spelled hopelessness.
There had been tests before, but not quite like this; there was
no holding on to anything. A spiritual group or spiritual orientation had long ago disappeared with everything else. I was
completely on my own in every aspect, as if I had been
dropped into an inner and outer desert. A. H. Almaas points to
this when he mentions that one loses any orientation and
direction at the latter stage of the search.[44] This of course goes
against the very grain of the idea of personal growth.

Of course, I just could not avoid but try and cling to the hope of
some orientation. I had conversations with a Jungian psychologist in order to see if there was anything in my unconscious
that I had missed, and this did not lead anywhere either. Nothing seemed to function like before, and the last thing I could
do was be still. The way I was perceiving things from the
inside was that it was like losing any coordinates around which
I used to orient myself, and I fought it, afraid of drowning. For
months, I woke up in a state in which the usual sense of self
seemed to have gone out the window. It felt as if I was spin-

ning in space, with everything turned upside down and inside out, and nobody I talked to could relate to it. Just very recently I came across a sentence that I wrote during this time: 'I feel lost without orientation in a white-out, except that it is like a grey-out.' Every painful aspect of my upbringing and conditioning also resurfaced during this time—all as if I was being played with by a life that refused to give me any hint as to the rules of its game or my role in it.

In a most wonderful and touching account about the inner journey, Irina Tweedie speaks about this phase: "The dark night of the soul is really the inner moments of utter dejection. Because what happens on the mystical path — the meditation is easy ... The Beloved is near ... It's all wonderful. The next day I am alone. I can't find the Beloved. God doesn't exist. It is awful. We call it the yo-yo syndrome — up and down, and up and down, and up and down, endlessly. And that provokes a kind of loneliness, and a kind of frustration, which St. John of the Cross calls the dark night of the soul. And as you can compare spiritual life to a spiral, the experiences repeat themselves in a higher and higher spiral, or rather higher and higher frequencies. The dark night of the soul gets deeper and deeper and deeper. I remember at the end I was practically suicidal.... When the mind is completely desperate, at one moment it sort of stops in the middle, utterly helpless. And it is in this moment that so-called illumination can come."[45]

The Mirrors Are Failing

There was one winter about two years into this phase when, 'by accident,' I came across some books by A. H. Almaas, including his *Point of Existence*.[46] The latter is a discussion of developmental psychology in which Almaas shows that the ego structure is fundamentally narcissistic, and that the origin of the sense of 'I' lies in it being mirrored by an object, the 'other.' As such, the 'I' is the self-representation within the psyche, the other pole of object-representation, and it cannot exist without the object reflecting it.

When this structure of self-representation starts breaking down, as happens in (and is the goal of) spiritual practice, Almaas explains how a number of unpleasant phenomena occur as a result. This runs somewhat counter to the widely accepted notion that spirituality brings more peace or nice states by default. Amongst the phenomena Almaas observed with his students who approached the root of self-representation, or the root of the 'I,' are sudden explosive anger, deep despair, depression, being unreasonably 'ego centered,' and others. In other words, those symptoms are rather the opposite of what everyone imagines the result of inner work to be.

Reading this gave me, for the first time, a frame of reference for what was happening. What was being described in modern psychological terms had been called the 'dark night of the soul' in the past. It may sound pathetic, but the sense is that God's light is shining everywhere except where 'I' am. In this phase, the object—the mirror in which the 'I' is mirrored—completely withdraws from oneself. It is bearable that people-objects or thing-objects go away, but it is most unbearable when the divine light and love also go away. Slowly, the subject is being brought down by the disappearing object. When the automatic 'survival' need of the 'I,' its mirror object, goes away, the root of the 'I' gets pulled because they coexist.

The ego structure is narcissistic because the 'I' cannot exist without seeing itself through the mirror of an object. That object can be an actual person or an interior representation, or any kind of self-definition, including a spiritual one. Looking at oneself through the mirror of a concept, including a spiritual one, keeps the 'I' alive. Mirroring oneself through any conceptualized 'other,' including a teacher, master, or the divine itself, keeps the 'I' propped up as well. Letting go of this mirroring throws one into absolute aloneness that can truly be like a dark abyss.

Recognition

Somebody may wonder what happened. From the point of view of the person who exists in time and space, there was a specific point in time when the mind stopped its usual functioning. Or rather, it was brought to a point where an accidental giving up occurred, where the conditions catalyzed a dropping into the unknown. But from the point of view of the revelation of true nature, from the point of view of the existential answer to the question of 'who am I,' it is clear that the person together with its concept of time was only a phenomenal manifestation, it was never real. It is like being catapulted out of identification with the 'small me' into a different realm. That 'small me' never was, only the source is. The 'small me' takes no credit for this because it could not have brought this realization about, in fact, it could not help but resist every attempt at its dissolution.

There was a concrete situation that prompted an intense bout of questioning, or discerning, something that my mind was used to doing, and sometimes compulsively so. Like a thousand times before, it ran in circles, but this time, something snapped. It was like becoming unconscious, and although the body did not fall from the chair it was sitting on, everything disappeared, including any trace of being conscious of anything. Then there was some small glimmer, awareness being aware of itself, but no objects, no self, nothing in it. There was an absolute unshakable certainty that beyond this, there is nothing to be wished for, to be discovered, to be known. With it came the knowing that this was always here, nothing ever happened to it, and that it is the source of all, of all that is, of all universes including that which is called the divine, or God.

In the past, I had come across the word 'absolute' and it had been the most mysterious of all spiritual terms, the olympic platinum medal of attainment. In other words, conceptually, it was 'absolutely' impossible to have an idea about the absolute, and this was the case—*it is the case.* More recently, a few years later, I read these words from Almaas' *Indestructible Innocence*: "If the Absolute is experiencing Absolute, the experience is that there is no experience.... It is absolutely empty of anything you can call experience.... I am not conscious of anything ... It is similar to deep sleep.... You are gone, absolutely gone.... It is the level of existence, of beingness, where there is not even the perception of beingness. You are beingness.... You cannot be driving a car and be ... in the Absolute, because in the Absolute you do not see a car.... The ultimate nature of things is a complete absence of all that can be experienced ... it is an absence of consciousness of anything. That is the ultimate source—the origin."

There was, as I came out of it, a very keen awareness of an indescribable dimension of reality. I understood for the first time why this has been likened to deep sleep. I had heard previously that samadhi is like deep sleep and had wondered how this could be in any way attractive—'I am doing all this spiritual seeking for a state in which nothing ever happens, for something as boring as deep sleep?' But in a hard-to-describe way, that is exactly the salvation. In deep sleep there is no awareness of any particular manifestation. It is being itself as of yet undivided, without there being consciousness of any object. At that level, there is not even light being born yet, let alone the usual 'I as body-mind' consciousness. Awareness arises out of it, as a kind of light which precedes the existence of time and space. There is no subject and object and hence no movement; no thinking, no feeling, no experience, only undivided eternal oneness, eternal because there is no time at that level. In a hard to describe visual way, it is the most luminous pitch dark blackness imaginable, being it rather than experiencing it.

The source is where all appearance and manifestation springs from. In itself, it seems more like absolute nothingness or the absolute void which gives birth to all that is, and all that is pours forth from it without beginning or end. The knowing that beyond this, there is nothing more that could be searched for was first hand and immediate. This knowing did not depend on any previous knowledge, it did not depend on anyone or anything, it did not depend on any psychological condition, on the notion of becoming or being something or someone, and did not depend on anything that happens in time. There is no condition for it. It is not the result of a time-based cause and hence is not a continuity of something. It is always, if anything, the cause of perceived continuity.

In hindsight, it seems strange to have believed that it had been missing, or why there was such desperation. In reality, it is most natural; it cannot be missed at all because it is always and everywhere. One knows it because it is evident to itself. It depends on nothing but itself, and especially on no one who is awake. Doubts do not arise as they belong to the mind, just as self-congratulation or feelings of achievement do not arise. There is simply no mind at that level.

The End of Longing

This self realization is not just another nice, powerful, or intriguing state like some of the ones which can happen on the inner journey. It does not go away. This is why it is not a state, because a state can change into some other state. Being at source is the precondition for all states. States belong to the manifest person. The source precedes all manifestation and is the same undivided *One* that underlies everyone and everything, whether it is known or not.

All this amounts to a qualitative and distinct leap in perception; as if the perception is moved from the head to the feet for the first time. But the body and its operating systems, its personality features, may not change—awakening is not about change.

There are people who might say 'you had a spiritual experience, good for you.' No, this is not another experience in a long succession of life experiences. An experience implies that there is an experiencer and something that is experienced—it belongs to the level of duality. There is no experiencer and nothing experienced in this. The experiencing, the observing, the watching subject, all fall back into pure subjectivity (another term for source). There is no one there anymore to have an experience.

This realization is also not an insight because insights depend on a perceiving subject whereas this knowing is immediate, impersonal awareness being home in itself. There have been discussions about whether it is a gradual or sudden happening, and I am favoring the latter, it being a very distinct cognitive leap. Some meditation teachers say there can be moments of enlightenment which then disappear, and I believe they are referring to the sense of 'am-ness' which always shifts into mind activity again. Some people liken 'realization' to expanded states, when the logical mind or emotional body temporarily loosen their grip; but again, expanded states belong to the mind.

All this just goes to show the extent to which the belief that spiritual growth is about experiencing great states, becoming someone else, or making changes, is such a prevalent notion. Basically, it is looking in the wrong direction. All such movements within time are revealed as illusions or the great play of maya. The outlook on how the world is perceived and how one perceives oneself shift because for the first time, it is possible to clearly see what the mind really is. For lack of a better expression, I call it a shift in perspective, but the word change or even transformation is not the right one in this context. One sees, for the first time, through the veils of a host of different self-concepts, the most fundamental of which is the notion of having, or being, an 'I.' This is the absolute end of the search, and when I say absolute, I do not mean it in the sense of a great spiritual term. It simply means any inner seeking has ceased for good, although on occasion I still seek my car keys or other things.

11

A Play without Actors

The Impact of Realization on the Mind

Afterwards, for quite some time, I had the sense that the real work starts here. Prior to this, the work is like trying to look at your own eyes, trying to look back at the same apparatus that does the seeing in the first place. This is a metaphor of the paradox, but it is just as paradoxical when applied to inner seeing.

There was, and is, a sorting out process—old beliefs trying to hang on like dry leaves in a storm. John Wren-Lewis describes his own aftermath in the following way: "There have been plenty of problems adjusting to awakened life ... my own resurrected mind still contains programs based on the assumptions of that state [of separation]."[47] I also did what Wren-Lewis proceeded to do. For the first time in years I sought out some contemporary teachers, but had to realize that there is nothing to ask when the costume of the seeker has been shed. For a while, the complete naturalness of the recognition made the mind want to compare it to ideas it held previously, and this may be what prompted writing the notes which led to this text.

Since then, the body-mind has continued to function according to its laws, the way it always has. It likely does not come across as different. I used to be convinced that I could 'feel' if another was really awakened—it was one of 'those' ideas; but nothing changes in the manifest. The body-mind is to a large extent, a collection of habits, and they do not disappear just like that, only the one who believed she can or should be transformed has now retired. Preferences that were formed on a physical-emotional level are still there. There is still the preference of tofu over pork, and if it was the other way round, it would neither prove nor disprove the likelihood or unlikelihood of the eater being awakened.

There are thoughts, feelings, memories, insights, and sensations, but the identification with them has dissolved because the 'I' to whom they can belong cannot be found. This is something I could not imagine before. It does not mean being adorned by an aura of the divine, or being surrounded by a halo. Others will hardly notice any special light, and most likely, they will continue to assume that they are someone and that others are also someones. There are movements of the body-mind and these are now experienced more like impersonal functions instead of the activities of an 'I,' which is what they always were.

Things are still happening, but there is now an immediacy to whatever is—there is no longer a need to look for psychological patterns beyond what arises in consciousness, and initially, this was a bit surprising. This also applies to the way 'others' are perceived—what is seen is seen. The need to figure things out, such as psychological causes and effects, has pretty much disappeared: why is there anger; is it appropriate or inappropriate; should there be more anger? There are moods, and sometimes there are none, but whatever is, I cannot attach any self-definition to it. In a strange way, neither waking, sleeping, nor dreaming affect the 'who I am'—the source of it all always is and cannot be found in either one.

Practical aspects of life do not necessarily shift. Still, whatever the appearances of the outer life, there is a knowing from where the silent benediction originates. Whatever ripples occur in the form of irritations are now less of a disturbance because they are on the surface. This does not mean everything is always rosy or joyful. It is rather that there are fewer filters—everything is funnier and more tragic at the same time.

I don't necessarily know how to lead 'my' life better, rather, life is leading itself through this temporary body-mind as well as through the totality of all other body-minds and everything else that is; and that life reveals itself from one moment to the next. I do not wear a constant enraptured smile; there is no constant anything. But everything is more factual; when there is an emotion, it is either expressed or not. There is no need to look for reasons beyond the fact. This sometimes reminds me of the little kid who goes on asking 'Mommy, why ...?' and after a while, mom only repeats 'Because, because ...' Instead of the automatic 'What? Why?' the prevailing sense is "This. Because."

The Difficulties of Labeling What Is

Silence, presence, emptiness, fulfilment, being and source—all have been used as synonyms for the 'truth' of who we are. In that sense, silence is not opposite to noise, but rather what precedes noise and is never disturbed by noise. How much a term is stressed depends on the particular spiritual theory. For example, some people seem especially drawn to theories in which 'silence' is something ultimate. Some spiritual traditions, particularly the Sufis, emphasize silence less than others, but a dervish still finds the point of stillness at the very center of his whirling. For me, 'silence' never had the connotation of being something supremely desirable; I was rather drawn to methods that were lively and feeling-based. Being attracted to silence can be a matter of personal preference or can be the result of a tendency towards avoidance. For example, an enneagram nine type personality may shy away from all perceived conflict and will try to hold on to peace and silence. According to Dawna Markova's personality model,[48] people who are auditory at a deep level need silence in the sense of 'absence of noise' to thrive and regenerate, while others prefer to have the radio playing during the whole day.

At the core of self, there is stillness because no movement between subject and object can be detected. This silence cannot be fabricated or brought about. It is not part of the eternal pendulum of finding oneself in turmoil/tension and desiring some relief. This stillness does not depend on suppressing movement, denying that which moves or is noisy, or the holding back of emotions or thoughts. It is what one is at the core. To look for it on the outside means not recognizing one is it. One cannot say one is enlightened or that one has found stillness. That notion would be based on a relative claim where stillness is seen in comparison to that which moves or is agitated.

Like silence, presence is not a point in time, whether chronological or psychological time. The now which is talked about as leading to truth is not a moment really; it is not a part of time. It is a bit confusing sometimes to people who aspire to be 'in the now' because they feel they are missing so many 'now' moments and then try to play catch-up, maybe even getting exasperated after trying. Sometimes there is also the expectation that the intention to be in the now will change something in the inner condition, consequently, there is frustration about the lack of a permanent result. This can be partly because the focus is on what arises in the 'perceived moment of now' and less on the 'who' for whom it arises. 'That which one is' always precedes time and anything that comes about within it; it is not possible to fall outside of the it—the 'now' is inescapable, everything is always now.

Language has its limits and its use may cause certain confusions. For example, the word presence can also be used in a non-temporal sense in a phrase such as 'there is only presence.' This may give the impression that presence is a something that is somewhere else other than the standpoint of the speaker, setting up a subtle misconception of separation. But whatever is, one is it.

Some traditions put a lot of emphasis on emptiness, and consider it something desirable, or of particular value. Emptiness usually refers to the sense of spacious 'am-ness' that can be experienced when mind activity ceases. It can occur by itself, or be brought about when one is in a state of awe through which the mind simply falls silent. From the viewpoint of the mind, this 'am-ness' is transcendent. However, even from the viewpoint of common sense, it is easy to see that the experience of it in its pure form does not last. Even before there was ever a search, or any meditation, I must have fallen in and out of emptiness a thousand times.

One can enjoy spacious 'am-ness,' but as soon as there is trouble with the car, or the spouse, or the children and one has to deal with specifics, it reverts to the background. It is true that in the experience of pure 'am-ness' there is no thinking, but one cannot function permanently on that level, it constantly morphs back into fullness and then the reverse. Meditative or silent retreats are a setting in which it is possible to open up to that sense of 'am-ness' to a greater extent than in daily life. But if its experience is taken for the goal, there may be a sense of losing a perceived higher state already on the way home, when concrete details of travel need to be attended to. Focusing too much on emptiness, it can be possible to become oblivious to what is happening in the surroundings, for example concerning interactions with and between people.

From the viewpoint of 'am-ness,' awareness is transcendent, and awareness does not consider emptiness or fullness as being higher or lower. Or, to put it another way, when there is no reference to an 'I,' it does not matter what is momentarily appearing. From the viewpoint of awareness, source is transcendent, being the cause for everything including awareness. Recently, I read how someone described their healing work by saying 'this work will connect you to the source'; but the whole notion of 'connection' is wrong because you are not two. You are the source, whether it is cognized or not, whether it is veiled or not.

Dropping the veil is equivalent to leaving behind the 'I' perspective. But when one hears statements such as 'the I is really not,' or 'the ego has to die,' or that there is 'no one' or 'no person,' this can trigger fear because the mind may translate this into 'I don't exist.' On a psychological level, many people have experienced a version of being very hurt when they felt overlooked, the common anguish being, 'it's as if I don't exist for him/her!' Not existing therefore comes across as a deep fear associated with a rather hurtful condition—how can there be anything fulfilling about being a nobody? One may prefer not to venture there, but if looked at in a calm way, it is clear that one's being is the condition for everything that arises in it, including every concept of 'I' and 'mine.' In a similar way, we often say that we don't feel 'understood', and this is also usually experienced as a hurtful situation. But who we are is exactly that which can never be understood; it is beyond understanding.

The 'I' idea gets started by being born in a body. Subsequently, everyone supports each other's 'I' ideas, most often through an unreflected inner mechanism of opinions about oneself, the world, and the other. One such idea is that consciousness/awareness lives in a body, or maybe the brain. Jean Klein speaks about the tendency for everybody to constantly locate him or herself as a conditioned reflex.[49] I remember once walking down the street and there was an awareness that 'I' am not inside this walking body and that the walking body is appearing 'within me,' with the 'me' being perceived as the vast space itself—awareness itself cannot be localized. From the vantage point of popular opinion, this sounds pretty mad and it may even be viewed as the psychological pathology of being dissociated from oneself. But it was no such thing—it was, and is, a very clear and present perception.

Whatever attributes are given, words can at best hint at a direction in which to look. That which is meant by 'source', or sometimes being, is the ultimate absence of anything concrete and definable. Nothing can be known about it because there is nothing knowable in it. Whatever can be distinguished from anything else is not it, but has been born out of it. From there, everything is a dream. When someone dreams that he falls into water while fully clothed, when he or she wakes up, the pyjama is not wet. Likewise, whatever unfolds in the phenomenal realm never affected one's being.

The Other Disappears with the 'I'

The concepts of 'I' and 'other' appear and disappear together. I have occasionally heard people say that they see, or try to see, the divine in another, but who has ever seen another? There is a body which is seen through the visual sense, behaviors that are observed, or an energy quality that is experienced by the intuitive sensory equipment. So the assumption may then be that these are steered by a personal entity who is producing them. When the locational orientation of consciousness as dwelling in one's own physical body ceases, the distinction between inside and outside, or self and other, ceases as well.

When we are not blinded by the fictional 'I' concept, the recognition that the other is also not a separate 'I' happens automatically. Cognizing source is at the same time the cognition that it is the source of all; no intellectual gymnastics are needed for this. The source is the same, but the manifestations which spring from it are manifold. There are still humans with their particular behaviors, and sometimes these behaviors evoke responses or even reactions from other organisms, just like bouncing a pebble on water causes ripples, nothing is separate from anything else. So if there can never be two, the idea of a personal relationship cannot be upheld—only two separate beings or things can relate. But letting go of the idea of relationship goes completely against the grain of what everyone has learned.

One such perceived 'relationship' is, for example, the dynamic between a teacher and another individual who then assumes the counterpart of student or disciple. The varied expressions of such interactions are as manifold as the individuals involved, the practice or method they gravitate to, their psychological make-up, their life circumstances and so on. For some, the dynamic is full of challenges, for others, it consists of a gentle guidance based on mutual amiableness. In some cases it is rooted in the concrete and mundane, in others, what transpires happens beyond words or in very subtle realms.

Whatever the characteristic, this is a very individual phenomenon, so the following remarks are very general. The first is made with regard to what is called an idealistic transference. In both the East and West, people have traditionally been more devotional, indeed, whole cultures could be devotional. The modern psyche has lost a bit of this innocence. What comes into play is that we often feel inferior and imperfect, and in order to avoid dealing with such perceived and painful inferiority, we project an ideal onto another. This idealizing means that for the wounded psyche, the 'other' (often the teacher) needs to be perfect, superior, or more divine. It is one's own need for psychic balance which creates this projection. If it is later found out that the other is not a divine god but a human who is not all that perfect, there can be quite an adverse reaction, or disappointment.

In this context, sometimes perceived others are idealized as holy, and many contemporaries even adore Ramana Maharishi as the perfect Advaita saint. The question arises if such ideals may not be projected, and if they are not images that exist only in the mind. If one happens to fall in love with the vibration of such a person, what one falls in love with is one's own origin which is forgotten. But Advaita means that all manifestations arise from the One, even those who are perceived to be a little less perfect. If a perceived other is defined as more holy, one defines oneself automatically as lesser, through that very definition. One would hope that spirituality can be freed from such self-inflicted hierarchies. The second remark in this context is to what extent the concept of 'spiritual teacher' includes a projection and a hope that there is something which one can get from the outside, that the teacher can give what is yearned for. But who one is cannot be given by a perceived other. And in that context, even the inner need for loving attention needs to drop away at one point.

I remember hearing a story about a Zen monastery where the master chose as his successor, a disciple who had spent thirty years in the kitchen cleaning rice and had never gotten so much as a single glance from the master. Another example is from the diary of Irina Tweedie where she talks about spending many afternoons waiting in the heat in front of her teacher's house while he simply ignored her for days on end, throwing her into deep despair. The 'I' can only exist when it is mirrored by an other, and not being mirrored, cherished or taken as important by the teacher or master can be especially hard to bear, as happens in times when the device of 'ignoring' is being used to break the 'I' identification.

Leaving the 'I' behind means entering absolute aloneness that is so absolute it may truly be frightening. There are no friends and enemies anymore, no fathers and bosses, mothers and lovers; no teachers, teachings, nor gurus, and no God. One has to give up absolutely the need to be mirrored by another, and no one seems to do this voluntarily. There is a saying that when you meet the Buddha on the road, kill him—which in my view is a way of saying that the mirror needs to disappear, and a master, or God, is the deepest representation of the coveted mirror object. Some say it is a quantum leap, but it is not the 'I' that does the leaping but rather one is leapt when the time is right.

The One Source

In Advaita, source is called 'One', or 'one without a second,' or 'not two'. Here, I only want to note that this 'one' falls outside of any numbering, it precedes it—it is beyond it. Many old and recent Advaita texts talk about how that 'one', also called source or absolute, relates to phenomenal experience.[50] They talk about how despite the perception of 'many', there is only one undivided being as the bottom ground. In other words, the source is transcendent, and it is also immanent, because whatever is cannot be other than it. One is what is, even when it appears otherwise.

What follows is that this 'one' is not out there, so that 'I' could then be a 'second'; it is simply who one is no matter what tradition or non-tradition someone subscribes to or in which words it is expressed. This fact does not depend on a cognition; it depends on no thing and is unconditional. In the absolute, nothing is distinguished yet, distinctions emerge from it, with the first one being the quality of God, light or awareness. This is found inside, and no scriptures are needed for it. Often, the goal and outcome of spiritual search is presented as divine light, eternal happiness, the great joy, or some other 'thing' and thus a slight misconception may be fed into: the belief that who one is can be found in a circumstance. But the question 'who am I?' intends to lead to the discovery that there is really never an answer, and this is the dissipation of both the question and the questioner.

The basic approach of Advaita confers the unsayable with only one Sanskrit word, but that unsayable is the ground of all religion and is expounded on in different traditions in varied and in sometimes lengthy ways. In realizing the nature of source, it is self-evident how what had been called God arises out of it, that there is no separate God either, and this may sound radical. The notion of 'oneness' can, however, act as a basic tenet, a belief or faith system, a kind of religion stripped of decorative elements. There is therefore a fine line between adopting it as a new dogma and trusting it as a gentle reminder about the direction in which to look. For example, knowledge about 'one' has now resulted in figures of speech in which references to 'I' are replaced with 'we.' This changes nothing when the 'I' is still the perceived center of functioning, and if one has not seen through the 'I' fiction, how can it be known who 'we' are?

If Advaita says it in one word, "tat tvam asi"[51] (thou art that) says it in three. Additionally, there are mountains of texts, from ancient scriptures to recent books, all attempting to explain the unexplainable. If it was a matter of simply reading, the phrase 'thou art that' would bring the cognition in two seconds. But it does not work that way, of course. By appearing as language, the not-knowable here also appears cloaked as something knowable. But maybe it can still be a sign post, who knows?

Endnotes

1. Ann Faraday, "Towards a No-Self Psychology."

2. Ibid.

3. John Wren Lewis, "Gnosis: Goal or Ground?"

4. Jean Klein put it this way: "[Love] stimulates itself by itself." Jean Klein, *The Ease of Being*, page 63.

5. See: Alexander Lowen, *Bioenergetics*.

6. See: Eric Berne, *Games People Play: The Basic Handbook of Transactional Analysis*.

7. Author of *Daughter of Fire*, a remarkable biography about her time with an unknown Indian Sufi guru. She became his disciple in her fifties and stayed with him for years in India until he left his body.

8. Irina Tweedie, in her interview with Dr. Jeffrey Mishlove: "Spiritual Training with Irina Tweedie."

9. See: Pupul Jayakar, *Krishnamurti: A Biography*.

10. Dynamic Meditation was created for the restless Western mind and includes stages of chaotic breathing, emotional release, stillness, and dance. For a description see, Osho, *Meditation: The First and Last Freedom*

11. Jean Klein, *The Ease of Being*, page 23.

12. See: Eckhart Tolle, *The Power of Now*.

13. Some say inner senses parallel outer ones, but whatever they are called, there is a quality that allows us to perceive both inner and outer workings/dimensions and that we can call awareness. Everyone notices thoughts more or less consistently, although they are not perceived with the outer senses.

14. Gurdjieff's movements of Sacred Dances are meant to increase attentiveness, while the Stop exercise is meant to bring awareness to what is going on in one's mind at that precise moment.

15. Neuro Linguistic Programming—developed by Richard Bandler and John Grinder.

16. Kirlian photography verifies energetic qualities by making them visible. Another example of the functioning of the intuitive layer is of someone not feeling good in a certain location as a result of being affected by its energetic quality.

17. An example is a German woman in her late fifties who had run a pub in former socialist East Germany, serving mostly meat and potato dishes, and beer. After the reunification of Germany, the pub was sold, the husband died, and a short while later, she started having experiences of a paranormal nature. She had never heard of such things, and had no idea what was happening to her until people who could put it all into perspective crossed her path, seemingly out of nowhere.

18. The despairing wounded condition of the psyche is well-described in *Facets of Unity, The Enneagram of Holy Ideas*, by A.H. Almaas.

19. Jean Klein (see: *The Ease of Being*) often refers to this openness as 'listening'—he was a musicologist. Others use 'seeing,' or 'being,' or 'noticing.'

20. Jean Klein, *The Ease of Being*, page 47.

21. See, Don Flory, "The Pearl Beyond Price," in: *Yoga Journal*.

22. John Pendergrast, "Psychotherapy: The Sacred Mirror," in *ONE: Essential Writings on Non-Duality*, ed. Jerry Katz, p. 121–130

23. John Prendergast, "Psychotherapy: The Sacred Mirror," page 128.

24. Osho, *The Book of Secrets*, page 232.

25. The kind of trauma that is referred to here is psychological and not medical trauma.

26. The notion of an 'Indigo person' was coined relatively recently. Observation has shown that about 20 particular behavioral and personality traits show up in especially sensitized children and adults, in a combination which has not been explained by other personality models. The definition of Indigo implies that individuals who have these traits—amongst them more children than adults—are noted to have an elevated level of consciousness. See, for example, Kabir Jaffe and Ritama Davidson, *Indigo Adults: Forerunners of a New Civilization*.

27. Myers-Briggs, termed MBTI (Myers-Briggs Type Indicator), is a personality typology based on C. G. Jung's work.

28. See: H. A. Almaas. *Facets of Unity: The Enneagram of Holy Ideas*.

29. Some people are only familiar with the daily banalities dispensed by newspaper astrologers and will call it some kind of hocus pocus. It is not so widely recognized that astrology is an old science with a highly scientific and involved discourse.

30. Richard Tarnac, *Cosmos and Psyche: Intimations of a New World View*, page 209.

31. The latter, as noted, for example, by Sri Karunamayi, a traditional devotional Hindu woman who is said to be enlightened.

32. See: Susan Segal, *Collision with the Infinite*.

33. Dr. Wayne W. Dyer, *The Power of Intention: Learning to Co-Create Your World Your Way*, page 118.

34. Ibid, p.113.

35. I neither recommend nor don't recommend any method. As far as therapeutic processes are concerned, there are a number that have been part of my path, and maybe a few will be on someone else's path. While reviewing the conceptual implications of a method, there is no judgment about the therapists who are involved with the methods.

36. The idea of alignment is very popular in psycho-spiritual language; what does it actually mean? It presumes the 'I' is a like a machine that can be well-oiled and made to run smoothly.

37. For reference, see, http://www.quadrinity.com.

38. As the word 'coaching' became more well-known in Germany, its ideological implications were imported together with it. Those ideas are basically touted in much the same way as they are in the US (see, for example, the books by Bodo Schaefer), with substantial disregard for cultural differences.

39. *Panta rei*—everything flows.

40. There are three aspects of God in Hinduism—Creator, Sustainer, and Destroyer; none exists without the others.

41. See: Csikszentmihalyi, Mihaly. *Flow. The Psychology of Optimal Experience.*

42. Like other healing methods I had encountered, this method increasingly sought to subsume every living phenomenon under its theoretical reach, trying to explain every thing and every occurrence.

43. Sufi mystic Rabi'a Al-'Adawiyya, also called Rabia al-Basri, was an 8th century woman from Basra, Iraq. It is said that she once searched for a needle outside the house and when someone asked her where she had lost it, she answered "inside," to illustrate how people search in the wrong place.

44. A.H.Almaas, *Indestructible Innocence*, page 158

45. Irina Tweedie: "Spiritual Training with Irina Tweedie". *Thinking Allowed*. Conversation with Dr. Jeffrey Mishlove.

46. A. H. Almaas, *The Point of Existence.*

47. John Wren Lewis, "Gnosis: Goal or Ground?" *Gnosis.*

48. See, Dawna Markova, *The Art of the Possible: A Compassionate Approach to Understanding the Way People Think, Learn and Communicate*. In this book, everyone is described as kinesthetic, visual, and auditory based on different levels of inner processing.

49. Jean Klein, *The Ease of Being.*

50. See, for example, the Heart Sutra, and particularly the comments of Wei Wu Wei on the Heart Sutra in: Wei Wu Wei: *Open Secret*. See also the recent compilation by Jerry Katz: *One. Essential Writings on Nonduality.*

51. A famous quote from the *Upanishads*.

Bibliography

Almaas, A.H. *Facets of Unity, The Enneagram of Holy Ideas*. Boston: Shambhala Publications, 2002.

Almaas, A.H. *Indestructible Innocence*. Boston, Shambala Publications, 1987.

Almaas, A.H. *The Point of Existence. Transformations of Narcissism in Self-Realization*. Boston: Shambhala Publications, 2000.

Berne, Eric. *Games People Play: The Basic Handbook of Transactional Analysis*. New York: Ballantine, 1996.

Csikszentmihalyi, Mihaly. *Flow. The Psychology of Optimal Experience*. New York: Harper & Row, 1990.

Dr. Dyer, Wayne D. *The Power of Intention: Learning to Co-Create Your World Your Way*. Carlsbad, CA: Hay House, 2004.

Faraday, Ann. "Towards a No-Self Psychology." *Consciousness*. June 1993. http://www.angelfire.com/realm/bodhisattva/faraday.html#N10.

Flory, Don. "The Pearl Beyond Price". In *Yoga Journal*. September/October 1990. http://www.ahalmaas.com/essence/flory.htm

Jaffe, Kabir, and Davidson, Ritama. *Indigo Adults: Forerunners of a New Civilization* Lincoln, NE: Iuniverse, 2005.

Jayakar, Pupul. *Krishnamurti: A Biography.* New York: Harper & Row, 1986.

Katz, Jerry. *One. Essential Writings on Nonduality.* Boulder, Co: Sentient Publications, 2007.

Klein, Jean. *The Ease of Being.* Durham, North Carolina: Acorn Press, 1984.

Lowen, Alexander. *Bioenergetics.* New York: Penguin, 1975.

Markova, Dawna. *The Art of the Possible: A Compassionate Approach to Understanding the Way People Think, Learn and Communicate.* Newburyport, MA: Conari Press, 1991.

Osho. *Meditation: The First and Last Freedom.* New York: St. Martin's Griffin, 1997.

Osho, *The Book of Secrets.* New York: St. Martin's Griffin, 1998.

Prendergast, John. "Psychotherapy: The Sacred Mirror." In: Katz, Jerry. *ONE: Essential Writings on Non-Duality.* Boulder, Colorado: Sentient Publications, 2007.

Segal, Susan. *Collision with the Infinite.* San Diego, CA: Blue Dove Press, 1996.

Tarnac, Richard. *Cosmos and Psyche: Intimations of a New World View.* New York: Viking Penguin, 2006.

Tolle, Eckhart. *The Power of Now.* Vancouver, BC: Namaste Publishing, 1997.

Tweedie, Irina. *Daughter of Fire.* Inverness: Golden Sufi Center Publishing, 1995.

Tweedie, Irina. "Spiritual Training with Irina Tweedie". In: *Thinking Allowed.* Conversation with Dr. Jeffrey Mishlove. http://www.intuition.org/txt/tweedie.htm

Wei Wu Wei. *Open Secret.* Boulder, Co: Sentient Publications, 2004.

Wren Lewis, John. "Gnosis: Goal or Ground?" *Gnosis.* Winter 1995.

Acknowledgments

I want to thank Julian Noyce from Nonduality Press who took an interest in this project in the early stages, and gently nudged me on at certain junctures. Also, many thanks to Jerry Katz, author of "One" and owner of nonduality.com who encouraged me and provided priceless assistance by sharing information. Above all, I thank Chris Dube from *Urban Mystic Books* for the dedication he showed when editing this text. I truly admire his artistry with language. I thank all other reviewers, as well as those who have taught me over the decades, and the many with whom a part of the path was shared.

About the Author

Dhyan Dewyea was born in Germany and graduated from the University of Heidelberg. After becoming an educator at the undergraduate level, she turned away from academia and studied body therapy. Late in her twenties, she traveled to India on a spiritual quest. Later, she worked in the travel industry for 14 years as an international tour group leader and interpreter. She trained in kinesiology, NLP and other methods of inner development, including coaching. She led coaching seminars in Germany for an institute of Professional Education. She has divided her time between Germany and the US. During the last year, she lived mostly in silence and relative seclusion under the big sky of the American West, and says that 'this can change any moment'. For further information, please visit: www.beyond-the-I.com

978-0-595-45901

0-595-45901-3

Printed in the United Kingdom
by Lightning Source UK Ltd.
129427UK00001B/80/A